D0423153

366 readings from
HINDUISM

THE GLOBAL SPIRIT LIBRARY

366 readings from
HINDUISM

edited by

ROBERT VAN DE WEYER

THE PILGRIM PRESS
CLEVELAND, OHIO

ARTHUR JAMES
NEW ALRESFORD, UK

First published in USA and Canada by
The Pilgrim Press,
700 Prospect Avenue East, Cleveland, Ohio 44115

First published in English outside North America by
Arthur James Ltd,
46a West Street, New Alresford, UK, SO24 9AU

Copyright © 2000 Arthur James Ltd

Translation, compilation and editing
© 2000 Robert Van de Weyer

05 04 03 02 01 00   5 4 3 2 1

The right of Robert Van de Weyer as translator, compiler
and editor of this work has been asserted in accordance
with the Copyright, Designs and Patents Act 1988.

All rights reserved.
Except for brief quotations in critical articles or reviews,
no part of this book may be reproduced in any manner
without prior written permission from the publishers.

A catalogue record for this book is available from
the Library of Congress and the British Library.

North America ISBN 0-8298-1388-8
English language outside North America ISBN 0 85305 451 7

Typeset in Monotype Joanna by
Strathmore Publishing Services, London N7

Printed by
Tien Wah Press, Singapore

CONTENTS

SERIES INTRODUCTION

The Global Spirit Library is the first comprehensive collection of the spiritual literature of the world, presented in accessible form. It is aimed at people who belong to a particular religious community, and wish to broaden their spiritual outlook; and at the much larger group, perhaps the majority of people in the world today, who have little or no attachment to a religious community, but seek spiritual wisdom. Each book contains the major writings of one of the world's spiritual traditions.

Much of the world's spiritual literature was designed to be read or heard in small portions, allowing ample time for personal reflection. Following this custom, the books in The Global Spirit Library each consist of an annual cycle of daily readings. Two or more books may be read in parallel at different times of the day; or an entire book may be read straight through. Again following a time-honoured practice, many of the original texts have been condensed.

Spiritual traditions differ from one another in their theological formulations; and the history of humankind is blighted by rivalry between different religious communities. Yet theology is no more than human speculation about truths that are beyond the grasp of the human mind. The writings in these books amply demonstrate that, as men and women actually experience these truths within themselves and others, divisions and rivalries fade, and unity is found. May the third millennium be an era of spiritual unity across the globe.

INTRODUCTION

Hinduism means 'the religion of the India'. A Hindu may be defined as someone who regards the ancient sacred texts of India as authoritative – and by this definition there have been Hindus from every nation and continent.

The Hindu religious tradition began with the arrival of Aryan people from central Asia about three and a half millennia ago. They adopted some of the religious ideas of the previous civilization which had flourished in the Indus valley in north-west India; and gradually they developed a religion of their own. From an early date there were two quite distinct kinds of religious leader: priests, who performed religious rituals, and whose office passed from father to son; and sages, who had acquired great spiritual wisdom, and whose advice and insights were eagerly sought. Frequently a sage attracted a community around him; and the community might survive his death, preserving his sayings either by oral repetition or in written form. These written records are the kernel of Hindu sacred literature.

THE VEDAS

The *Vedas* were composed over several centuries after about 1200 BCE. The term 'veda' means sacred knowledge; and the *Vedas* are said to be based on direct communication from the divine to Hindu sages.

The most ancient and famous of the *Vedas* is the *Rig Veda*, a collection of more than a thousand hymns. They are about God and addressed to God in various forms; and they are filled with startling images and paradoxes. They were recited at acts of worship — the word 'rig' denotes a priest's chant. The last of the *Vedas*, the *Atharva Veda*, is personal, consisting of meditations and incantations which individuals can use.

The God of fire

I pray to the God of fire, the God of the sacrifice, the one whose chants and hymns bring greatest blessing.

The God of fire inspired the ancient sages to pray, and he inspires the sages of the present time to pray also. He surrounds us with divine blessings. Through the God of fire we may win wealth and health; we may have many offspring, whose actions will make us proud.

The sacrificial rituals which the God of fire demands, encompass every aspect of our lives. The rituals are effective: whatever blessings the God of fire wishes to bestow on his worshippers, will be bestowed.

We come day by day to the God of fire, offering to him our thoughts and our hopes. He shines in the darkness of our minds. We can reach him as easily as children can reach their parents. He dwells among us, and makes us happy.

Rig Veda I: I. I–4, 6–7, 9

The cosmic tree

No being is equal to you, God of nature, in sovereignty and power. No being is equal to you in courage. No bird can fly as swiftly as you can. No river can move with such force as you do. No mountain can stand as firmly against the raging wind as you can.

You are a cosmic tree whose roots are at the bottom of the deepest ocean, whose top supports the sky, and whose branches spread across the entire universe. And you also grow within each living creature.

You fashioned the sun, and you steer it through the sky. You give feet to those who are lame, and you bring peace to anguished hearts. You give the power of healing to a hundred thousand men and women. You ward off illness, and protect us from ageing before our time. You deliver us from the bonds of sin.

You set the stars in their places, to form constellations for all to see. Where do they go by day? You have made laws which are clear in meaning and purpose. At night the moon rides into the sky, displaying her beauty.

We praise you with sacred words, and we offer sacrifices to you, in the hope that you will bless us. God of nature, do not be angry with us. We strive to obey your laws; do not rob us of life.

Rig Veda 1:24.6–11

The dawn

Look at how the dawn has set up her banner on the eastern horizon. She has adorned and anointed herself with sunlight. She is throwing lights of red and gold into the sky.

She is singing as she sets about her work. She has come from a distant place on a chariot drawn by tawny cows, who emit a soft light. She brings food day by day to those who act righteously, to those who are generous, and to priests who perform their rituals with care.

Like a dancing girl she decorates herself with bright ornaments. She uncovers herself, revealing breasts as swollen as those of a cow ready to be milked. From her breasts come light that fills the entire universe. She breaks out of the darkness, as cows break out of their pens.

Her brilliant flame becomes visible once more. She pushes forward, driving back the formless darkness of the night. She gazes out at all the creatures of the world, and sends her light straight into every eye. She awakens all that lives – and she gives words to every poet.

This divine being is born again and again each morning, always dressed in the same colours. She causes men and women to grow older, pulling them across their span of life. She is a cunning gambler whom no one can outwit.

She pushes aside her sister, the night, beyond the very edges of the sky. And she draws to herself her lover, the sun.

Rig Veda 1:92.1a, 2a, 3–5a, 10–11

Three divine strides

I shall proclaim the heroic deeds of the God of light. In three strides he can cross from one end of the earth to the other. His home is in the highest mountains, where he wanders freely like a ferocious beast. Every creature lives within the space he can cover in three paces.

May the God of light hear this hymn, and be inspired. As he strides across the world like a vast bull, crossing every land and sea in three steps, may he hear my words.

His three footprints are filled with divine honey. The footprints are so deep that the supply cannot be exhausted. When we drink the honey, we rejoice. With his first step he holds up the sky; with his second step he keeps the earth in place; with his third step he guides every living creature.

There is a place where men and women worship the God of light with unceasing devotion; it is the home of joy. These men and women form the family of the God of light; and they live on the honey which overflows from his deepest footprint. I long to go to that place.

Rig Veda 1:154. 1–5

The sky and the earth

The sky and the earth are essential for all life. They make the laws by which all creatures exist; and together they have given birth to the sun, who is the great poet of space. They are the father and mother of all that lives; and in the space between them all creatures are conceived. The sun moves along the course which they have set.

The father and mother are vast and strong and tireless. They protect the entire universe. The Creator has made them as shapely as adolescent girls, and dressed them in the brightest clothes.

The great poet of space, who is their favourite child, is immensely clever. He understands everything with perfect clarity, and he dispels the darkness of ignorance and folly.

The Creator fashioned the sky and the earth, which are essential for all life. He measured out the space between them, and fixed them in their places with pillars that can never decay.

We sing hymns of praise to the mighty sky and the mighty earth. We rejoice in their glory and their power, and we promise to live according to their laws.

Rig Veda 1:160.1–3a, 4–5

The female and the male principle

Some say the one who created the universe is female; some
say that the one who created the universe is male. Those who
have eyes, can see the female and the male; but those who
are blind, cannot understand. The poet, who is the offspring
of the parents of creation, knows this well; thus the poet becomes the parents' parent.

   Those who encounter the parent beneath the sky, which
is above, and the parent above the earth, which is beneath –
those with such mystical insight can proclaim the source from
which the divine mind comes.

Rig Veda 1:164.16, 18–19

The tree of knowledge

Two birds, who are friends, perch on the tree of knowledge, the tree of immortality. One of them eats the sweet fruit. The other looks on without eating. The birds sing, without blinking, of how they will share immortality with the wise.

The bird who eats the sweetness, will nest and brood on the tree of knowledge, the tree of immortality. That bird will learn that the fruit growing on the tips of the branches, is the sweetest. And it will also learn that in order to eat this fruit, it must come to know the parent of creation.

Rig Veda 1:164.20–22

One God with many names

The four quarters of the sky reach down to the oceans on the edge of the universe, and from there the waters flow. The whole universe is sustained by the divine syllable, Aum, which flows everywhere.

Speech is divided into four parts. Three parts are used only for mystical discourse; the fourth part is used in normal conversation.

People refer to God by many different names. God is like a bird who flies everywhere. The wise know that God is one, yet appears in many forms. So they know that all the names have the same meaning.

Water is evaporated by the flaming sun, and rises up in the sky; water returns as rain to enliven the earth. The same water appears day by day in different forms.

The great bird with wonderful wings, the beautiful embryo of all living things, the water that causes all things to grow – they are God, and I call to God for help.

Rig Veda 1:164.42, 45–46, 51–52

God's insight and power

God had insight from the beginning; and from the beginning the power of his thought has given protection to all beings. Whenever God breathes, the sky and the earth tremble at his power. Believe in God, my people.

At first the earth was tottering and the mountains shaking; God set the earth on firm foundations, and made fast the mountains. He propped up the sky, and filled the space between the earth and the sky with air. Believe in God, my people.

People sometimes ask: 'Where is God?' Or they say: 'God does not exist.' Yet he can destroy the wealth of the world as quickly as a gambler can lose his money. Believe in God, my people.

God gives strength to the weary, comfort to the sick, and food to the hungry. Every horse and every cow is under his command. He made the villages in which the common people live, and the chariots on which the warriors ride. At dawn each morning he gives birth to the sun. Each day he causes the sea to rise and fall. Believe in God, my people.

When two armies confront one another in battle, the warriors of both invoke God – as do the priests on either side. No army can win victory without his help; so he decides which army will win. He himself can be defeated by no one and nothing. Believe in God, my people.

Rig Veda 2: 12. 1–2, 5–6a, 7–9

The divine leader

Let my song to the God of nature exceed in greatness every song that has ever been composed. Let me exercise perfect control of my mind, that my verse is perfect. I sing to the God of nature, whom I love to worship, and who adores all who adore him.

We praise you with our thoughts, God of nature. We awake each morning like kindled fires, committing ourselves anew to do good. May we find joy in serving you.

You protect us, and you give us courage; you are our leader, and your voice inspires us. When we are tied by the rope of sin, you loosen it and set us free. You take us to the spring from which righteousness flows.

As I weave this song, do not let the thread break. Do not let my work end before its fulfilment.

Banish all fear, O God of nature, and hold me fast. Set me free from all anguish, as a calf is set free from its tether. I cannot bear to live apart from you even for the blink of an eye.

God of nature, when I have committed a sin, I search for you. Do not punish me with your weapons; do not exile me from your light. Wash away the stain of evil, that I may live.

God of nature, the homage that was paid to you long ago, I pay now – and I shall continue to pay in the future. Your laws are an unshakeable mountain, and you cannot be deceived; upon those laws I build my life.

Rig Veda 2:28. 1–8

Daily prayer

We meditate on the beautiful light of God; may it stimulate our thoughts.

Rig Veda 3:62.10

Divine healing

God of storms, the medicines which you have given me, have healed my body of a hundred fevers. The medicines which you have given, have cast hatred and anguish from my soul. You drive away every kind of disease.

You, God of storms, are the glory of all glories, the strength in all who are strong. You carry the thunderbolt in your hand. Carry us across the seas of danger to the further shore. Ward off every kind of attack.

We do not wish to provoke your anger by worshipping you in the wrong way, or praising you with the wrong words, or by invoking other spiritual powers. We know that, of all healers in the world, you are the best. Make us heroes in your sight.

Where is your merciful hand, God of storms, that can cool the hottest fever, and can remove all spiritual sickness? Have mercy upon me. Your medicines are so pure and so powerful; they ease every kind of pain. No wonder the parent of all humanity turned to you for happiness and health! We also turn to you.

Divert your weapons of anger; suppress your fury towards us; loosen the bow that is aimed at us. Be our only patron, our source of bounty. Have mercy on our children and grandchildren.

Rig Veda 2:33.2–4, 7, 13–14

Divine anger

The God of nature, who gives wisdom to every generation, supports the sky and the earth – despite their vastness and their weight. He has pushed the sky upwards, and stretched it out to form a dome. He has pushed the earth downwards, and unrolled it. And he has set the sun on its double course, moving above the earth by day and below the earth by night.

I ask my heart: 'When will the God of nature show love towards me? Why do my offerings provoke him to anger? Why does he not enjoy my offerings? When shall I see his mercy, and rejoice?'

I ask myself what sins I have committed. I want to understand what I have done wrong. I turn to the wise, and ask them to enlighten me. But they merely tell me what I already know: that I have provoked the God of nature to anger.

O God of nature, what was my terrible crime, that now causes you to destroy me? I am your friend, praising you constantly. Tell me at once, that I may prostrate myself before you, begging forgiveness. I know that you cannot be deceived, and that you are your own master.

Rig Veda 7:86. 1–4

Freedom from sin

Free me, God of nature, from the sins of my ancestors, and from the sins that I myself have committed. Free me from the diseases and misfortunes that are the consequences of sin. I am like a tethered calf; cut the rope, and set me free.

I have never committed a sin deliberately; I have never intended to do wrong. Wine, anger, gambling, and stupidity have led me astray. My older relatives have lured me to follow their evil ways. Even sleep does not ease my guilt.

As a slave is happy to serve a generous master, I should be happy to serve you – even though you are angry with me. In your wisdom you give wisdom to the unwise; and when the unwise become wise, they quickly prosper.

O God of nature, you are your own master. Let my devotion to you lodge itself in your heart. Pour out your blessings, that all might go well for me.

Rig Veda 7:86. 5–8

Plea for mercy

God of nature, keep me away from the house of clay, the place of death. I am not yet ready to go there. Have mercy upon me, great ruler, have mercy.

My body and limbs are swollen with disease. I wobble and tremble, like a wineskin filled with air. O master of the earth, have mercy upon me; great ruler, have mercy.

If through weakness of will I have tried to swim against the current of your will, have mercy upon me. You alone are pure. Great ruler, have mercy.

Even though I swim in your waters, a terrible thirst overwhelms me; a spiritual fever overcomes me. I struggle to sing your praise. Have mercy upon me, great ruler, have mercy.

If as a mere human I have offended you, do not punish me. If through stupidity I have violated your laws, do not injure me. Have mercy, God of nature.

Rig Veda 7:89. 1–5

The ruler of the world

If I were like you, O God, and ruled alone over the wealth of the world, I should treat with respect all who treated me with respect. I should do my best for everyone; and especially I should honour those who are wise, recognizing that they possess great spiritual power.

But you, O God, are ruler. No one, neither a divine nor a human being, can obstruct your generosity to those who worship you and offer you gifts. Our worship makes you grow greater in our eyes. We know that you rolled out the earth, as a carpet on which to walk; and you made the sky as your crown. We ask your help, because your greatness is without limits, and you possess all wealth.

When you drank the sacred drink, you went into an ecstasy; and in that ecstasy you created the atmosphere between earth and sky. Then you set the stars in the sky, securing them firmly in their places, so they cannot be pushed away.

Your love constantly moves forward, like a wave on the ocean; your joy gives light to all whom you rule. Our hymns and songs of praise remind us of your greatness, O God; and when we sing them, you make us happy.

Rig Veda 8:14.1–2, 4–7a, 9–11

Worthy of praise and worship

You are not small, O God; you are not a child. You are great and powerful. Therefore you are worthy of praise and worship.

Protect us, help us, and speak on our behalf. Do not lead us away from the path of Manu, the first human being, the father of all humans.

You are everywhere. You belong to every man and woman. You reach out to all of us, and to our cows and horses, and give shelter.

Rig Veda 8:30. 1–2a, 3–4

The drink of life

I have tasted the sacred drink, the sweet drink of life, knowing that it inspires good thoughts and instils good feelings. Every living being desires it, for it is the essence of sweetness.

When you have drunk the sacred drink, you penetrate the soul. You discover that the soul has no limits. By penetrating the soul, you avert the divine wrath; and you enjoy the friendship of God. You become like a docile cow, on which God puts his yoke.

We have drunk the sacred drink, and we have become immortal; we have gone to the source of light; we have entered the divine home. What injury can befall us now? What harm can the hatred and malice of others do to us?

The sacred drink is kind and gentle, as parents are kind and gentle to their children. The sacred drink is considerate, as one friend is considerate to another. May the sacred drink stretch the span of life.

The glorious drops that I have drunk, have set me free, so that I can move where I want. The sacred drink has bound together the parts of my body, as thongs bind the parts of a chariot. Thus the sacred drink protects me from injury, and prevents my foot from stumbling.

The sacred drink has inflamed my heart, so that it blazes like a fire. Its light enables me to see far; its warmth is wealth itself.

Rig Veda 8:48. 1–6a

The guardian of the body

Sacred drink, have mercy upon us, and preserve our health. We who drink you, are devoted to your laws. You stir up passion for justice, and fury against oppression. Do not allow our enemies to overwhelm us and use us for their pleasure.

You, sacred drink, are the guardian of the body. You watch over us, and you dwell in every organ and limb. If we break your laws, have mercy on us; continue to treat us as your friends; help us to act better in the future.

You are our closest friend; your compassion is boundless. When we have drunk you, we are safe from all injury. When you flow through our bodies, God stretches out the span of our lives.

All weakness and disease have gone; the forces of darkness have fled in terror. You have entered us, and are pervading every part of us. You have reached our hearts; your immortality has penetrated our mortality. The span of life stretches before us without end.

As you extend across the earth and the sky, you bring every creature into unity; a single drop of your holy liquid bestows peace. Every creature will worship you; and you will make every creature rich.

Speak with a clear voice. Do not let us rest from serving you. Never allow us to utter lies or slander. Let every word we say, and every deed we do, be an act of worship.

Rig Veda 8:48.8–12a, 13–14

The God of truth

You try to grab the God of truth, but he slips away. You try to overpower him, but he overpowers everything. He possesses all the wisdom of the wise, and all the visions of the poets.

He gives clothes to the naked, and heals the sick. Through him the blind see and the lame walk. He defends those who are persecuted – whether or not they brought the persecution on themselves. By his intelligence and skill he drives away evil from the sky and the earth.

Those who seek the God of truth, find him. He is generous to those who are generous to others; but he stops the greedy from getting what they want. Those searching for ancient knowledge which has been lost, find it. He guides and encourages all who strive to penetrate his mysteries; and he stretches out their span of life.

Be kind and merciful to us, God of truth. Be gentle with us, and do not take us up into the whirlwind of your powers. King of truth, do not enrage us or frighten us; do not injure us with your dazzling light. Give us only the help that we need. Drive from us all hatred, and protect us from failure; thwart every evil plan.

Rig Veda 8:79. 1–9

Different abilities

Our abilities fit us for different occupations, and cause us to seek different opportunities. Those with ability in carpentry, seek furniture that is broken, so they can mend it. Those with ability in healing, seek bones that are fractured, so they may mend them. Those with ability in spiritual matters, seek patrons who will support them in their pursuit of wisdom. They all serve God in their diverse ways.

We seek the materials and tools for our occupation. The smith, for example, seeks wood for his fire, the feathers of large birds to fan the fire, flat stones on which to place the molten metal, and hammers to press the metal into shape.

I am a poet. My father is a physician, and my mother is a miller. With our different abilities we strive for wealth, as a cow seeks lush grass. We all serve God in our diverse ways.

The harnessed horse longs for a light cart; the seducer longs for a woman's smile; the penis longs for two hairy lips; we long for God.

Rig Veda 9: 1 1 2. 1–4

Water of life

Water, you are the one that brings us life. You are the source of nourishment that gives us strength. We rejoice at your existence.

We drink you with joy, as babies drink their mothers' milk. And when we swallow you, we receive love – as babies receive love from their mothers.

You bring us to birth and you give us life in the service of God. So let us go straight to the house of God. You keep us happy and healthy in the service of God. May God always be our help and our preserver.

You are the mistress of all things and the ruler of all people. When we are sick, we beg you to cure us. You are our armour, protecting us from illness. We pray that we shall continue to see the sun rise for many years.

Water, carry away all my sins and my failures, all that has been bad in my life. Cleanse me of deceit and malice and broken promises. I seek you today; I shall plunge into your wetness. Drown me in splendour.

Rig Veda 10:9. 1–5, 7–9

The living and the dead

Go away, death, by your own path, which is different from the divine road. You have eyes, so you can see me; and you have ears, so you can hear me. Do not injure our children or our adults.

Mourners, wipe away the footprints of your funeral procession; wipe away the footprints of death. Let the span of your life stretch before you, growing longer and longer. Become pure and clean, so your worship will be acceptable to God. May you have many children, and always be prosperous.

Those who are now dead, have parted from those who remain alive. Dance and laugh, as dancing and laughing stretches the span of life.

There is a wall between the dead and the living, so the dead cannot return. May the living survive for a hundred years. The dead will remain dead, and their bodies will remain silent beneath the earth.

As one day follows another, and as one season follows another, one generation follows another. Let the young care for the old, and never abandon them. Everyone must eventually climb onto old age.

Rig Veda 10:18.1–3a, 4–5

Restraining grief

Women who are not widows, and who have good husbands, make your complexions shine with butter. Be free of sadness and sickness. Dress in beautiful clothes, and climb into the marriage bed with joy.

Women who become widows, rise up, and return to the world of the living. Do not remain with a man from whom the breath of life has departed. In the past he took your hand, and desired your body; but now he has gone. Say to him: 'You are there, and I am here.'

Earth who receives the dead, do not crush them. Be gentle with them as they enter you. Wrap them up, as a mother wraps up her child in the edge of her skirt.

A day will come when each one of us will be laid in the earth, as a feather is stuck into a cleft in an arrow. When that day comes, may the mourners restrain their grief, as they restrain a horse with a bridle.

Rig Veda 10:18.7–9a, 11, 14

A sick person's soul

If your soul is about to go to one of the four corners of the earth, we beg your soul to remain here, dwelling within you.

If your soul is about to go to one of the four quarters of the sky, we beg your soul to remain here, dwelling within you.

If your soul is about to go to the surging ocean, we beg your soul to remain here, dwelling within you.

If your soul is about to go to the beams of light in the sky, we beg your soul to remain here, dwelling within you.

If your soul is about to go to the sun, or go to the place from which the dawn rises, we beg your soul to remain here, dwelling within you.

If your soul is about to go to the high mountains, we beg your soul to remain here, dwelling within you.

If your soul is about to merge into the entire universe, we beg your soul to remain here, dwelling within you.

If your soul is about to go to that which is beyond the beyond, we beg your soul to remain here, dwelling within you.

If your soul is about to go to what has been and what is to be, we beg your soul to remain here, dwelling within you.

Rig Veda 10:58.3–6, 8–12

The gift of speech

When the poets and sages first set speech in motion, giving names to all things, they wished to make plain the pure and perfect secrets of the world; and they were prompted by love.

When the poets and the sages fashioned speech out of thought, sifting words as grain is sifted through a sieve, they enabled friends to express their friendship. They designed speech as a channel of love.

The poets and the sages offered speech as a gift to all people. Some looked at the gift, but could not see it. Some listened to the gift, but could not understand it. But to some the gift revealed itself, as a loving wife undresses and reveals herself to her husband.

Those who abuse the gift by speaking falsehoods, are like milkless cows. Those who prefer lies to truth, are like trees with no blossom or fruit. Their friendships are awkward and tense, providing no encouragement in the contest of life.

Those who are faithless and disloyal, abandoning their friends when it suits them, lose the benefits of speech. What they hear, they hear in vain, for it does not lead to goodness or wisdom.

Rig Veda 10:71.2–6

Sharing knowledge

All people have eyes and ears, but their insight and under-standing are not equal. Some people are like shallow ponds, that reach only to the shoulder or mouth; and some people are deep lakes, in which others can immerse themselves.

When people gather for worship, some have nothing to say, because they do not know the object of worship; and some overflow with praise, because they know the object of worship in their hearts.

Friends should encourage one another in the contest of life. They should save one another from error by sharing their knowledge – just as they should save one another from hunger by sharing their food. They should push one another forward to win the divine prize.

There are many ways of sharing knowledge. Some people can compose poems like trees, in which each line is a branch bearing the blossom of divine truth. Some can sing songs, whose melody and rhythm are the music of divine love. Some can repeat the words of ancient sages. Some can perform the ancient rituals.

Rig Veda 10:71.7–8, 10–11

God's base and material

What was the base on which God stood, when he sculpted the world? What kind of raw matter comprised the base on which God stood, when he stretched out the sky in its glory? Who made the base on which God stood, when he cast his eye on all that he had made?

With eyes on all sides, and mouths on all sides, and arms on all sides, and legs on all sides, the one God created the sky and the earth, fanning them with his arms.

From what kind of wood did God fashion the earth? From what kind of tree is the sky carved? Sages, search your hearts to discover the base on which God stood when he sculpted the world.

O God, show us the highest places in which you dwell; show us the lowest places; and show us the places in between. Help us to see these places when we worship you. O God, you obey your own laws. You offer sacrifices to yourself to make yourself strong.

Creator of all, you have made yourself strong, by offering to yourself the earth and the sky. Other people may wander hither and thither, not knowing which way to turn; but we look towards you as our rich and generous patron.

We pray to you, Creator of all, the lord of speech and the inspirer of thought. Help us in the contest of life. You are the maker of all good things, and you are generous to all living creatures. Listen to our prayers with favour, and help us.

Rig Veda 10:81. 1–7

The Creator and his creatures

The Creator of the sun, whose heart is wise, gave birth to the earth and the sky in the form of purified butter. They bowed to him in worship. He fastened them both in the east, and then moved them apart.

The Creator of all is vast in mind and vast in strength. He fashions things, and sets them in order. He is the example which all living creatures should follow. When they pray to him, and make sacrifices to him, he fills them with joy. He dwells beyond the constellations.

He is our father. He fashions all things and all worlds, and sets them in order. He gives names to every kind of creature. And all creatures can ask him questions.

Singers offer him their songs, and the rich offer him their wealth. All who are wise, offer him what they possess.

But he cannot be found; the Creator cannot be known by those whom he has created. Ignorance has divided the Creator from his creatures. Even those who recite hymns in his honour, are glutted with pleasures, so their minds are filled with mist, and the words on their lips are empty.

Rig Veda 10:82. 1–4a, 7

The primal man

The primal man has a thousand heads, a thousand eyes, and a thousand feet. He pervades the earth in all directions, and extends beyond the earth by the length of ten fingers.

The primal man is all that is, all that has been, and all that will be. He is the ruler of immortality. This is the measure of his greatness. Yet he is even greater than this. All creatures on earth are only a quarter of him; three quarters comprise those beings who are immortal in heaven. Three quarters of him rose to heaven, while only a quarter stayed on earth; and from there he spread out in all directions, permeating all living beings and all material objects.

From him woman was born; and from her man was born. From his mouth priests were born; from his arms rulers were born; from his thighs craftsmen were born; and from his feet labourers were born.

From his mind the moon was born; from his eye the sun was born; from his breath the wind was born. From his navel the atmosphere was born; from his head the sky was born; and from his ear the four quarters of the sky were born. Thus the universe was set in order.

Rig Veda 10:90. 1–2a, 3–5a, 11b–13a, 14

The work of priests

Be of one mind, you priests, for you share the same spiritual nest. Harmonize your thoughts: weave them together like the warp and weft on a loom; let them move to a common rhythm like the oars on a ship. Sharpen your thoughts, as if they were weapons to be used in battle.

You are horses, and your rituals are ploughs; so harness the ploughs to the horses. You are sowers, and your prayers are seeds; so scatter the seeds on the ground which your rituals have prepared. Sing a hymn as you plough and sow; then you will harvest a rich crop of blessings.

You are ropes, your rituals are buckets, and your prayers are the well. The water of divine love is never exhausted. So let the buckets be lowered and drawn up, that all may enjoy the water.

You are horses, and your rituals are chariots; so harness the chariots to the horses, that the race may be won. Let the chariots be vehicles of good fortune.

Rig Veda 10:101.1a, 2b–3, 5, 7a

The value of generosity

God did not ordain hunger as the way for people to die. He ordained that people should be well fed, and die by other means.

The wealth of those who give generously, never runs out. But when the miser's wealth is exhausted, no one shows compassion.

When the poor come to you in great need, begging for food, do not harden your hearts against them. Remember that the poor may once have been rich, and you may one day be poor.

When you see people who are thin for lack of food, beg them to accept your help. Put yourself at the service of those who call at your house seeking help; remember that you may need their friendship in times to come.

Those who do not share their food with their friends, are not true friends. Those who are mean to the companions at their side, are not true companions. Drive away false friends; rid your home of false companions. Let them look elsewhere for friendship; let them seek companionship amongst strangers who do not know them.

Let those who are strong, protect those who are weak. The strong should remember that, as they walk the path of life, they will weaken. Riches roll from one place to another, like the wheels of a chariot.

Rig Veda 10:117.1–5

Two feet and two hands

Those who do not make friends, lack foresight; and they grow their food in vain. This is the truth; their lack of foresight will cause their death. By cultivating neither patrons nor friends, they leave themselves unprotected in times of need.

The plough that works the soil, puts food in your belly. The legs that walk, put the road behind you. The mouth that speaks the truth, is better than the mouth that remains silent. Those who give freely, are superior to those that keep their wealth to themselves.

The sun, which moves without feet, is greater than the human being, who moves on two feet. The young person on two feet moves faster than the old person on three feet – two feet and a cane. Babies on four feet come at the call of adults on two feet. So those on two feet must protect and serve all other creatures under the sun.

Two hands, though they belong to the same person, are not equal in dexterity. Two cows from the same mother do not give the same amount of milk. Twins do not possess the same abilities. And two members of the same family do not give with the same generosity.

Rig Veda 10: 117.6–9

Carrying oblations

I have been lifted high by the sacred drink, and am moving freely through the sky like the wind. Have I not drunk the sacred drink?

I have been energized by the sacred drink, and am galloping like swift horses bolting with a chariot. Have I not drunk the sacred drink?

I have heard the divine voice, as the calf hears the lowing of the cow. Have I not drunk the sacred drink?

I turn around the words of the divine voice within my heart, as a wheelwright turns the wheels of a chariot. Have I not drunk the sacred drink?

The great nations that dominate the world, are no more than specks of dust in my eye. Have I not drunk the sacred drink?

The sky and the earth cannot oppose my flight, because my wings are too powerful. My vastness surpasses the vastness of the sky and the earth. Have I not drunk the sacred drink?

I shall put the earth where I want, perhaps here or perhaps there. I shall thrash the earth into submission. Have I not drunk the sacred drink?

One of my wings touches the sky, and the other trails along the earth. I am carrying oblations to God. Have I not drunk the sacred drink?

Rig Veda 10:119.2–11, 13

The golden embryo

In the beginning the golden embryo arose. As soon as it arose, it became the source of all creation. It put in place the earth and the sky. Is the golden embryo the God whom we should worship?

From the golden embryo comes life and strength. All the other divine beings obey its command. Its shadow confers immortality – or death. Is the golden embryo the God whom we should worship?

The golden embryo is so powerful that it is lord of the world; it is the lord of all that breathes and blinks. It rules over two-footed creatures, and four-footed creatures. Is the golden embryo the God whom we should worship?

The golden embryo is so powerful that it possesses the snowy mountains. It possesses the vast ocean, and also the mighty river that encircles earth and heaven. It has two arms embracing the north, two embracing the south, two embracing the east, and two embracing the west. Is the golden embryo the God whom we should worship?

When two opposing armies face one another, their soldiers with trembling hearts look up to the golden embryo, and seek its help – and the golden embryo rises, and casts its brightness upon them. Is the golden embryo the God whom we should worship?

Rig Veda 10:121.1–4, 6

The power of speech

I am speech – and I am queen of the world. I am the point at which all riches meet. I am the point at which all skills come together. I have many parts, I dwell in many places, and I take many forms.

I am the one who knows what food to eat. I am the one who gives meaning to what is seen. I am the one who lives in every breath. I am the one who gives understanding to what is heard. Though they do not realize it, people eat, see, breathe and hear through me.

Those who are famous for their wisdom, are wise through me; I taught them what they know – and they heeded me. I am the one who conveys joy from one person to another. Those whom I love, I make clever and sharp.

I strike down those who hate to pray. I incite people to compete for knowledge. I have pervaded the earth and the sky.

At the summit of the world I gave birth to the parent of all living creatures. My womb is in the ocean, in the depths of the sea. I watch over all my descendants, and touch the sky with the top of my head.

I am the one who causes the wind to blow, embracing all creatures. I am beyond the earth and beyond the sky; my greatness cannot be contained.

Rig Veda 10:125.3–5, 6b–8

Neither existence nor non-existence

In the beginning there was neither existence nor non-existence; there was no atmosphere, no sky, and no realm beyond the sky. What power was there? Where was that power? Who was that power? Was it finite or infinite?

There was neither death nor immortality. There was nothing to distinguish night from day. There was no wind or breath. God alone breathed by his own energy. Other than God there was nothing.

In the beginning darkness was swathed in darkness. All was liquid and formless. God was clothed in emptiness.

Then fire arose within God; and in the fire arose love. This was the seed of the soul. Sages have found this seed within their hearts; they have discovered that it is the bond between existence and non-existence.

Who really knows what happened? Who can describe it? How were things produced? Where was creation born? When the universe was created, the one became many. Who knows how this occurred?

Did creation happen at God's command, or did it happen without his command? He looks down upon creation from the highest heaven. Only he knows the answer – or perhaps he does not know.

Rig Veda 10:129. 1–7

Long-haired ascetics

The long-haired ascetics hold fire within themselves; they hold every drug within themselves; they hold the sky and the earth within themselves. Their long hair proclaims their knowledge; through them people may find the source of light.

These ascetics are naked to the wind, protected only by a few rags. When the divine wind enters them, they fly in whatever direction it blows. Driven into holy madness by their austerities, they are lifted in spirit by the wind. An observer can only see their stationary bodies; but within their bodies a divine storm rages.

They sail through the air, looking down on the earth below. They are friends with every power, both divine and natural; they want every power to perform its function well.

They move through the air with the elegance of a youthful dancer, and with the agility of a wild beast. These long-haired ascetics can read the minds of all whom they encounter; and they excite every mind which they read.

Rig Veda 10:136.1–4, 6

The gale

Behold the power and the glory of the gale; he is like a mighty warrior riding a chariot. He smashes solid objects into pieces as he passes, making a noise like thunder. He touches the sky, leaving red streaks; he touches the earth, throwing up the dust.

The rain chases after the gale, like a woman chasing a man. She climbs onto his chariot, rejoicing that he is king of the universe.

Moving along in the atmosphere between earth and sky, the gale does not rest for a single moment. He is a friend of the ocean, and the original guardian of the divine law.

Where was the gale born? From what was the gale made? The gale is the divine breath, and the embryo of the universe. He goes wherever he pleases. He can be heard, but he cannot be seen. Let us worship the gale, submitting to his will.

Rig Veda 10:168. 1–4

Cosmic order and truth

Cosmic order and truth evolved from the heat which the Creator emits. Night and day, land and sea, and winter and summer arose from cosmic order and truth. Cosmic order and truth rule over every creature that blinks its eyes.

The Creator set the sun and the moon in their proper places. He set the earth and the sky in their proper places, and put atmosphere between them. Then he caused light and heat to shine from the sun.

Rig Veda 10:190.1–3

The first man and woman

Who formed the heels of the first man and woman? Who formed their flesh and ankles? Who made their nimble fingers? Who designed the man's penis to expel liquid and semen, and who made his testicles? Who designed the woman's vulva to receive his penis? Who gave them a sense of balance, enabling them to stand firmly?

From what materials were their ankles and kneecaps made? How were their bones inserted into their flesh, and how were their joints installed? Where were their joints made? Who can answer these questions?

To each body two arms and two legs were joined. To the arms hands were welded, and to the legs feet were welded. Above the knees flabby thighs and buttocks were added. Who produced them? How does the flesh attach to the bone?

Did one being or many beings make the first man and woman? Did one being or many beings form their heads and necks? How many beings designed their breasts and nipples? How many beings built their shoulders and ribs?

Who told the arms how to do heroic deeds? Who attached their shoulders to their bodies? Who bored the seven apertures in their heads – the ears, the nostrils, the eyes and the mouth? Who taught them how to use their senses, enabling them to understand and manipulate the world?

Who put the tongue between their jaws, and then instilled in the tongue the power of speech? Who showed them how to walk and swim? Who can answer these questions?

Atharva Veda 10:2.1–7

The work of God

Does distress and despair, melancholy and madness come from God? Does pleasure and prosperity, joy and reason come from God?

Was the human form, in all its beauty, designed by God? Does God give each person a distinct character and appearance? Does God give men and women the ability to think?

Does God give human beings the urge to worship? Does God plant the notions of truth and untruth in the human mind? Does God decide when human beings should die? Does God offer the hope of immortality?

Did God ordain that human beings should wrap their bodies in clothing? Did God devise the human way of life? Did God decree that humans should be strong and agile?

Did God spread the waters across the ocean? Does God make the day bright? Does God kindle the fires of dawn? Does God bring the darkness at dusk?

Does God plant the semen in men? Does God weave the foetus in the female womb? Does God guide children from folly to wisdom? Does God give men and women the capacity for music and dance?

Atharva Veda 10:2.10, 12, 14–17

The great priest

Through whom does God adorn the earth? Through whom does God rule the sky? Through whom does God make human beings greater than mountains? Through whom does God perform his works?

Through whom does God fill the clouds with rain? Through whom does God make people wise? Through whom does God guide human worship? Through whom does God teach human beings the truth? Through whom does God guide the human mind?

Through whom does God cause the sacred texts to be written? Through whom are people able to encounter God? Through whom does God make the sacrificial fires burn? Through whom does God make time pass?

Through whom is this earth held down, and the sky held up? Through whom is the atmosphere – this vast expanse between earth and sky – sustained?

The great priest is the divine head and heart. A wind rises through his brain, and is expelled from his crown. This wind fulfils all God's purposes. It is the breath of life, which sustains and nourishes all God's creatures. It carries God's thoughts.

Atharva Veda 10:2.18–21, 24, 26–27

The divine son

In which of the divine son's limbs does passion dwell? In which of his limbs is the divine law inscribed? Where is his power? Where in him does faith reside? In which of his limbs is truth established?

From which of the divine son's limbs does fire blaze forth? From which of his limbs does the wind blow? From which of his limbs does the moon emerge? Look at the mighty limbs of the divine son!

In which of the divine son's limbs does the earth abide? In which of his limbs does the atmosphere dwell? In which of his limbs is the sky stretched out? In which of his limbs can the realm above the sky be found?

For whom does the fire blaze, the wind blow, and the moon follow its course? For the divine son. For whom does the moon wax and wane, the seasons come and go, and the fruit swell and ripen? For the divine son. Who is he, and what is he?

Did the divine son exist in the past, and will he extend into the future? He has a thousand limbs, and can make a thousand more; so he can be wherever and whenever he wants.

Through the divine son we can understand the world and all that it contains, and we can understand the waters. We can understand both existence and non-existence. Who is he, and what is he?

Atharva Veda 10:7.1–5, 9–10

The breath of life

I pay homage to you, breath of life, for the whole universe pays homage to you. I honour you as the lord of all, for on you all things depend.

I pay homage to you, breath of life, rejoicing in the sounds you make; I pay homage to you in the thunder. I pay homage to you when you make lightning flash, and send rain from the sky. When storms rage, the plants conceive and form embryos – and new plants grow.

I pay homage to you, breath of life, when you come and when you go, when you stand still and when you sit. I pay homage to you when you inhale and when you exhale, when you turn away from us and when you turn towards us. To you, above all beings, homage is due.

Breath of life, your form is dearer to me than any physical form. I yearn for your healing touch, knowing that when you touch me, I am whole.

Breath of life, you take every living creature as your garment. You look upon every living creature as a parent looks upon a beloved child. You are lord of all that breathes, and all that does not breathe.

Breath of life, do not turn your back on me. Live in me, and I shall live for you. Dwell within me as an embryo dwells within the womb – that I may truly live.

Atharva Veda 11:4.1–3, 7–10, 26

THE UPANISHADS

The *Upanishads* are the words of spiritual teachers, recorded by their disciples; the term 'upanishad' denotes sitting close to a teacher. They are traditionally regarded as explanations of Vedic teaching, but philosophically they are far more profound; and their philosophy is mystical, with little concern for the outward forms of religion. They are a mixture of didactic discourses, theological speculation, spiritual meditations, and stories about teachers and their disciples. And since they are compilations from various sources, they move freely from one form of writing to another. They date from the middle centuries of the first millennium BCE. Their teachings have much in common with Buddhism; the Buddha was a spiritual teacher in India in this period – and if his community had not formed the basis of a global religion, his words could have fitted quite comfortably within the *Upanishads*.

Words at the start of worship

At the beginning of an act of worship, these words should be recited: 'From delusion lead me to truth. From darkness lead me to light. From death lead me to immortality.'

Death is delusion, and truth is immortality. So the first and last sentence have the same meaning.

Those who understand these words, have conquered the world. And those who have conquered the world, are free from all fear.

Brihadaranyaka Upanishad 1:3.28

The original soul

In the beginning there was a single soul. This soul looked around, and saw nothing but itself. It exclaimed: 'Here I am!' From that moment the concept 'I' came into existence. Realizing it was alone, this entity became afraid. Then it thought: 'Why should I be afraid, when there is no one but me?' So its fear subsided.

Yet, since pleasure can only be enjoyed in company, this soul lacked all pleasure. Thus it wanted a companion. It was as large as a man and a woman embracing. So it split into two, becoming a husband and a wife. That is why it is said that a husband and wife are two halves of a single being.

The husband and wife had sexual intercourse; and from their union human beings were born. She then thought: 'Since we came from the same soul, surely it is wrong for us to have intercourse. I shall hide myself.' So she became a cow. But he became a bull, and they had intercourse; and from their union cattle were born. Then she became a mare, and he a stallion; and from their union horses were born. In this way all living creatures were born, down to the smallest insect.

Thus the soul is the common vital entity in every living being. The soul is dearer than a son or daughter, dearer than wealth, dearer than all things. When people recognize that only the soul is truly dear to them, then that which is dear to them, will never perish.

Brihadaranyaka Upanishad 1:4. 1–4, 8

Trinity and unity

The universe is a trinity: name, form, and action.

The source of all names is the word, for it is by the word that all names are spoken. The word is behind all names; and God is behind the word.

The source of all forms is the eye, for it is by the eye that all forms are seen. The eye is behind all forms; and God is behind the eye.

The source of all actions is the body, for it is by the body that all actions are performed. The body is behind all actions; and God is behind the body.

While the universe is a trinity, it is also a unity; this unity is the soul, the spirit of all life.

The immortal is veiled by the real. The soul, the spirit of life, is immortal. Name and form are real; and by them the soul is veiled.

Brihadaranyaka Upanishad 1:6.1–3

The location of God

There was once a priest called Gargya, who was proud of his learning. He went to King Ajatasatru, and said: 'I am willing to teach you about God.' The king replied: 'I shall give you a thousand cows if you can do that.'

Gargya said: 'There is a soul in the sun which shines by day; and that soul I venerate as God.' The king responded: 'How can you say that? I regard the sun only as the source of brightness.'

Gargya said: 'There is a soul in the moon which shines at night; and that soul I venerate as God.' The king responded: 'How can you say that? I venerate the moon only as the source of wine.'

Gargya said: 'There is a soul in wind and fire, and that soul I venerate as God.' The king responded: 'How can you say that? I regard the wind as like an army, and fire as like a powerful empire.'

Gargya said: 'There is a soul in the sound of people as they walk, and in their shadows, and that soul I venerate as God.' The king responded: 'How can you say that? I regard the sound of people's steps as a sign of life, and their shadows as a sign of death.'

Gargya said: 'There is a soul in the human body, and that soul I venerate as God.' The king responded: 'How can you say that? I regard the body simply as the covering of the soul.' Gargya now fell silent.

Brihadaranyaka Upanishad 2:1.1–3, 6–7, 10, 12–13

The truth of truth

King Ajatasatru asked: 'Is that all you have to say about God?'
Gargya replied: 'That is all.' The king said: 'If that is all, then
you know nothing.' Gargya said: 'Let me become your pupil.'
The king said: 'It is contrary to custom that a priest should
be the pupil of a king. Nonetheless I shall teach you what I
know.'

The king arose, took Gargya by the hand, and led him to
a man who was in a deep sleep. The king shook the man, and
he awoke. The king asked Gargya: 'When this man was
asleep, where had his consciousness gone? And when he
awoke, from where did his consciousness return?' Gargya did
not know.

The king said: 'When you fall asleep, your consciousness
and your senses go to rest within the soul; the soul holds
within itself the powers of life – speech, sight, hearing and
thought. Then when you dream, your soul enters a world in
which your deepest desires can be fulfilled; you can be a great
king, or a wise priest, as you choose, and travel wherever you
want. We conclude that, as threads come from a spider and
sparks come from a fire, so from the soul come all the powers
of life and all worlds; all existence springs from the soul.
Thus the soul is truth; and to know the soul is to understand
the mystery of God, who is the truth of truth.'

Brihadaranyaka Upanishad 2:1.14–18, 20

The reality of love

One day a sage called Yajnavalkya said to his wife Maitreyi:
'The time has come for me to leave this worldly life. So I
shall divide my property between you and my other wife
Katyayani.' Maitreyi said: 'If I were to possess all the wealth
in the world, would it help me to attain immortality?' The
sage replied: 'Not at all. You would merely live and die like
any other wealthy person. No one can purchase immortality
with gold.' Maitreyi said: 'What is the point of giving me
something that will not make me immortal? I should prefer
you to teach me all that you know.' Yajnavalkya exclaimed:
'You have always been very dear to me; and now you say
something which is very dear to me. Come and sit beside me;
and as I speak, concentrate hard.'

When his wife was sitting at his side, the sage spoke: 'A
wife holds her husband dear, not of love for him, but out of
love for the soul within her. A husband holds his wife dear,
not out of love for her, but out of love for the soul within
him. Parents hold a child dear, not out of love for the child,
but out of love for the soul within them. People hold religion
dear, not out of love for religion, but out of love for the soul
within them. People hold the entire world dear, not out of
love for the world, but out of love for the soul within them.
Thus we should watch and listen to the soul; we should reflect and meditate upon it. When we come to understand the
soul, we understand all existence.'

Brihadaranyaka Upanishad 2:4. 1—5

Salt in water

The sage continued: 'No one can understand the sound of a drum, without understanding both the drum and the drummer. No one can understand the sound of a conch shell, without understanding the shell and the one who blows it. No one can understand the sound of a lute, without understanding both the lute and the one who plays it. As there can be no water without the sea, no touch without the skin, no smell without the nose, no taste without the tongue, no sound without the ear, no thought without the mind, no work without hands, and no walking without feet, so there can be nothing without the soul.

'When you throw a lump of salt into water, it dissolves; you cannot take it out again, and hold it in your hands. Yet if you sip any part of the water, the salt is present. In the same way the soul can be perceived everywhere and anywhere; the soul has no limit or boundary.

'At present there is duality. You perceive other beings: you see them, hear them, smell them, and think about them. Yet when you know the soul, and when you recognize that the soul within you is the soul of all beings, how can you perceive other beings? How can you see and hear them, smell them and think about them? How can you regard yourself as subject and other beings as objects, when you know that all are one?'

Brihadaranyaka Upanishad 2:4.7–9, 11–14

The light within the heart

Yajnavalkya went to visit Janaka, who was king of Videha. The king asked: 'What is our light?' The sage replied: 'The sun is our light, for by the sun we sit, work, go out and come back.' The king asked: 'When the sun sets, what is our light?' The sage replied: 'The moon is our light, for by the moon we sit, work, go out and come back.' The king asked: 'When both the sun and the moon have set, what is our light?' The sage replied: 'Fire is our light, for by the glow of fire we sit, work, go out and come back.' The king asked: 'When the sun and the moon have set, and the fire has burnt itself out, what is our light?' The sage replied: 'Speech is our light, for we can move towards the sound of a person speaking.' The king asked: 'When the sun and the moon have set, when the fire has burnt itself out, and when no one speaks, what is our light?' The sage replied: 'The soul is our light, for by the guidance of the soul we sit, work, go out and come back.'

'What is the soul?' the king asked. The sage replied: 'The soul is consciousness. It shines as the light within the heart. While remaining unchanged, the soul thinks and moves. The soul is in the world of waking life, and is in the world of dreams. When the soul takes on a body, it seems to assume the body's frailties and limitations; but when the soul sheds the body at death, it leaves all these behind.'

Brihadaranyaka Upanishad 4:3. 1–8

States of consciousness

The sage continued: 'As human beings we have two states of consciousness: one in this world, and the other in the world beyond. There is a third state between these two; in this third state we are aware of both worlds, with their sorrows and their joys.

'When we die, it is only the physical body which dies; we continue to have a non-physical existence, in which we retain the effects of our past lives. These effects determine our next life. During this period between lives we experience the third state of consciousness.

'In this third state of consciousness there are no chariots, no horses drawing them, and no roads on which they travel; we make up our own chariots, horses and roads. In this third state there are no joys and pleasures; we make up our own joys and pleasures. There are no ponds filled with lotus flowers, no lakes and no rivers; we make up our own ponds, lakes and rivers. That which we make up, is determined by the effects of our past lives.'

Brihadaranyaka Upanishad 4:3.9−10

Waking and sleeping

'When we are sleeping, the soul, which is always awake, watches our dreams by its own light. Our dreams are woven out of past deeds and present desires. During sleep the soul keeps the body alive with the breath of life.

'In our dreams the soul wanders wherever it wants. It assumes many different forms, eats with friends, has sexual intercourse, and sees many awesome spectacles. But the soul is not affected by anything, because it is detached and free. Thus after wandering from place to place, enjoying many pleasures, and observing both good and evil actions, the soul returns to its original state.

'A great fish swims between the banks of a river as it likes; similarly the soul moves freely between waking and dreaming. As an eagle, weary after soaring in the sky, flies down to its nest, folds its wings and rests, so the soul has a period of dreamless sleep, when it is free from all activity.'

Brihadaranyaka Upanishad 4:3.11–19

The supreme goal

'The soul in itself is free from desire, free from evil, and free from fear.

'When a man is in the arms of his beloved, he is oblivious to what is happening around him and within him. In the same way when we are in union with the soul, we are oblivious to what is happening around us and within us. In this state all desire is fulfilled, because union with the soul is the only desire; there can be no suffering.

'In this state there are no parents, no worlds, no spiritual forces, and no sacred texts. In this state there is neither thief nor murderer; there is no low caste or high caste; there is neither monk nor ascetic. The soul is beyond good and evil, and beyond all sorrows of the heart.

'In this state we see without seeing, smell without smelling, taste without tasting, speak without speaking, hear without hearing, touch without touching, think without thinking, know without knowing – for nothing is separate from us. Where there is separateness, there is a subject which sees, smells, tastes, speaks, hears, touches, thinks and knows; and there are objects. But where there is unity, there is no subject and no objects.

'This is divinity. This is the supreme goal of life, the supreme treasure, the supreme joy.'

Brihadaranyaka Upanishad 4:3.21–32

The process of dying

'A heavily laden cart creaks as it moves along the road; in the same way the body groans under the burden of life as death approaches. When the body grows weak through old age or illness, the soul loosens itself from the body, as a mango or a fig loosens itself from its stalk; and thus it prepares to begin another life.

'The soul gathers the powers of life to itself, and descends with them into the heart. As life leaves the eye, and returns to its source within the soul, the eye no longer sees. As life leaves the nose, and returns to its source within the soul, the nose no longer smells. As life leaves the tongue, and returns to its source within the soul, the tongue no longer tastes. As life leaves the mouth, and returns to its source within the soul, the mouth no longer speaks. As life leaves the ear, and returns to its source within the soul, the ear no longer hears. As life leaves the mind, and returns to its source within the soul, the mind no longer thinks. As life leaves the skin, and returns to its source within the soul, the sense of touch is lost.

'By the light of the heart the soul leaves the body; and as the soul leaves, the powers of life follow. Since the soul is consciousness, the body loses consciousness as the soul departs; and the soul carries the spiritual effects of all that the person has done, experienced and known.'

Brihadaranyaka Upanishad 4:3.35–36; 4.1–2

From one life to the next

'When a caterpillar has come to the end of a blade of grass, it reaches out to another blade, and draws itself over to it. In the same way the soul, having coming to the end of one life, reaches out to another body, and draws itself over to it.

'A goldsmith takes an old ornament, and fashions it into a new and more beautiful one. In the same way the soul, as it leaves one body, looks for a new body which is more beautiful.

'The soul is divine. But through ignorance people often identify the soul with the mind, the senses and the emotions. Some people even identify the soul with the elements of earth, water, air, space and fire.

'As people act, so they become. If their actions are good, they become good; if their actions are bad, they become bad. Good deeds purify those who perform them; bad deeds pollute those who perform them.

'Thus we may say that we are what we desire. Our will springs from our desires; our actions spring from our will; and what we are, springs from our actions. We may conclude, therefore, that the state of our desires at the time of death determines our next life; we return to earth in order to satisfy those desires.'

Brihadaranyaka Upanishad 4:4.3–6a

Freedom from desire

'Consider those who in the course of many lives on earth have become free from desire. By this we mean that all their desires have found fulfilment within the soul itself. They do not die as others do. Since they understand God, they merge with God.

'When all the desires clinging to the heart fall away, the mortal becomes immortal. When all the knots of desire strangling the heart are loosened, liberation occurs.

'As the snake discards its skin, leaving it lifeless on an anthill, so the soul free from desire discards the body, and unites with God – who is eternal life and boundless light.'

Brihadaranyaka Upanishad 4:4.6b

Finding the soul

'When people truly understand the soul, they proclaim: "I am the soul." What desires could such people continue to have? What anxieties could they possibly have about their bodies?

'When people find and recognize the soul within themselves, they realize that the soul is the Creator of all things, the author of the universe itself. They know that the world belongs to the soul – the world is the soul.

'We can find and recognize the soul even while we are alive on earth. And through finding the soul, we become immortal. But so long as we fail to find the soul, we must endure great suffering.

'When we perceive that the soul is divine – when we acknowledge the soul as the master of what was, what is, and what will be – all fear is dispelled. We rejoice in that perception, since it makes us immortal.

'The soul is the breathing behind breathing, the sight behind sight, the hearing behind hearing, the thinking behind thought.

'The soul has existed from before the beginning of time.

'Those who know the soul, realize that all is one. They realize that diversity is an illusion, and unity is truth. Those who see only diversity, and cannot see unity, wander from death to death.'

Brihadaranyaka Upanishad 4:4.12–15, 17–19

Knowing the soul

'The soul is not born, but always exists. It is the consciousness of life, and dwells in every heart; it is the master of all,
the lord of all. The soul is not made greater by good actions,
nor diminished by bad actions. It is the supreme sovereign,
and the protector of all living beings. It is the bridge between
this world and the world beyond; and it is also the dike
which separates them.

'Those who love God, seek the soul through studying the
sacred texts, through worship, through acts of charity, and
through abstaining from pleasures. Those who find the soul,
become sages. They demand nothing for themselves, because
those who know the soul, possess the whole world. They do
not desire offspring, and nor do they desire wealth; they regard all desire as empty.

'The soul cannot be defined; it is not this or this. The soul
cannot be comprehended, because it is beyond comprehen-
sion. The soul cannot pass away, because it is imperishable.
The soul is free, because it has no bonds of attachment. The
soul is serene, because it cannot suffer or fear suffering.

'Those who know the soul, feel no grief at the evil they
do, nor elation at the good they do; they are beyond good
and evil. They are indifferent to what is done and left undone.
They are masters of themselves, and they are utterly calm and
tranquil. They see the soul within themselves, and they see
the soul in all beings.'

Brihadaranyaka Upanishad 4:4.22–23

The teaching in thunder

The Creator had three kinds of children: angels, humans and demons. He taught them the sacred texts.

When they had completed their studies, the angels said to him: 'Teach us something more.' He replied with a single syllable: 'Da.' Then he asked: 'Do you understand?' They said: 'Yes, we understand. You told us to show restraint.' The Creator said: 'You have understood.'

The humans said to him: 'Teach us something more.' He replied with a single syllable: 'Da.' Then he asked: 'Do you understand?' They said: 'Yes, we understand. You told us to show generosity.' The Creator said: 'You have understood.'

The demons said to him: 'Teach us something more.' He replied with a single syllable: 'Da.' Then he asked: 'Do you understand?' They said: 'Yes, we understand. You told us to show compassion.' The Creator said: 'You have understood.'

Whenever thunder rolls, you can hear the sound: 'Da! Da! Da!' The Creator is repeating his teaching: 'Show restraint. Show generosity. Show compassion.'

Brihadaranyaka Upanishad 5:2.1–3

The syllable Aum

Aum – let us meditate on this syllable, which is the foundation of prayer.

The earth emerges from the waters; plants emerge from the earth; human beings emerge from plants; speech comes from human beings; and Aum comes from speech. Aum is the essence of all essences. It is the highest of the high. It is the ultimate.

Speech and breath combine to form Aum. Speech and breath are like a couple in coitus, and Aum is their offspring. Aum is the fulfilment of their desires.

The syllable Aum signifies assent, for we say it when we assent to something. And assent is nothing but fulfilment.

The syllable Aum is the call to knowledge. We sing the praises of this syllable, which is the key to every kind of knowledge.

Those who know the soul, and those who do not know the soul, stand side by side reciting this syllable. But knowledge and ignorance are quite different. Only when it is recited with knowledge and faith, and with awareness of the hidden connections, does it become truly potent.

Chandogya Upanishad 1:1.1–2, 5–10

Striving for truth

There are three types of people striving for truth. First, there are those who offer sacrifices, recite hymns, and undertake acts of charity. Secondly, there are those who abstain from all bodily pleasures. Thirdly, there are those who are students of a spiritual teacher, living permanently at their teacher's home. All three types can earn great merit; and if they are steadfast, they may attain immortality.

The Creator created the universe by meditating in tranquillity. From his meditation came three syllables: bhur; bhuvas; and suvar. Bhur is earth; bhuvas is space; and suvar is sky. He then meditated on these three syllables; and from them came the syllable Aum. As leaves come from a stem, all words come from the syllable Aum. The syllable Aum is the whole universe; Aum is the truth of the whole universe.

Chandogya Upanishad 2:23.1–3

The outer and the inner light

There are five ways by which we may perceive truth. The first is sight, which is symbolized by the sun. The second is hearing, which is symbolized by the moon. The third is words, symbolized by fire. The fourth is thought, symbolized by rain. And the fifth is breathing, symbolized by the wind. These are the five courtiers of God; they are the five doorkeepers of heaven. Those who know and understand these courtiers, are spiritual heroes.

There is a divine light, which shines from above the highest point in the universe. It illuminates all beings, and warms them. It is the same light which shines in the heart of every human being. When we touch a human body, we feel warmth; this heat comes from the divine light. When we press our ears shut, we hear the crackle of a blazing fire; this sound comes from the divine light. We should venerate this light, as we feel it and hear it. When the light shines brightly within us, our faces become radiant.

Chandogya Upanishad 3:13. 1–7

The size of the soul

The universe emerges from God, and will return to God; he is the beginning and the end. God is all, and all is God.

You are your deepest desire. Your deepest desire in this life will shape your next life. So direct your deepest desire to knowing the soul.

The soul can be known by those who are pure in heart. The soul is light and life, truth and space. The soul is the source of all activity, all desires, all fragrances and tastes. The soul is beyond words. From the soul comes eternal joy – and the soul dwells within every heart.

The soul is smaller than a grain of rice, smaller than a grain of barley, smaller than a mustard seed, smaller than a grain of millet, smaller even than the kernel of a grain of millet. Thus the heart has room for the soul. The soul is also larger than the earth, larger than the sky, larger than the entire universe.

Chandogya Upanishad 3:14.1–4

A living sacrifice

A human being is a living sacrifice. The first twenty-four years of a human's life constitute the morning sacrifice. During these years a human should pray: 'With divine help, may my morning sacrifice sustain my powers of life until I offer my midday sacrifice.'

The next forty-four years of a human's life constitute the midday sacrifice. During these years a human should pray: 'With divine help, may my midday sacrifice sustain my powers of life until I offer my evening sacrifice.'

The last forty-eight years of a human's life constitute the evening sacrifice. During these years a human should pray: 'With divine help, may my evening sacrifice sustain my powers of life until I offer my death.'

Those who lead good lives, and say these prayers, will live one hundred and sixteen years; and they will not suffer illness until death.

Chandogya Upanishad 3:16.1–7

The inner and the outer world

In the inner world of the soul, God is consciousness; and in the outer world God is space.

Think of God as four-legged. With respect to the inner world, speech is one leg, breath is the second, sight is the third, and hearing is the fourth. With respect to the outer world, fire is one leg, wind is the second leg, the sun is the third leg, and the earth is the fourth. The outer world may enter the inner world.

Consider speech: when fire enters speech, every word fills with sacred truth. Consider breath: when wind enter breath, every breath fills with sacred truth. Consider sight: when the sun enters sight, every sight fills with sacred truth. Consider hearing: when the earth enters hearing, every sound fills with sacred truth.

Chandogya Upanishad
3:18.1–6

The truthful disciple

A young man called Satyakama said to his mother: 'I feel the time has come for me to go to a spiritual teacher. The teacher is bound to ask about my family. So please tell me to what family I belong.' His mother replied: 'I do not know to what family you belong. When I was a young woman, I was very poor, and served as a maid to many masters. Then I became pregnant with you; but I do not know who was your father. My name is Jabala, and yours is Satyakama; so call yourself Satyakama Jabala.'

The young man went to a spiritual teacher called Gautama, and said: 'I want to become your disciple. 'To what family do you belong?' Gautama asked. Satyakama replied: 'My mother does not know the identity of my father. Since her name is Jabala, and mine is Satyakama, I call myself Satyakama Jabala.' The teacher replied: 'No one but a true servant of God could have said that. Go and fetch firewood, and I shall initiate you as my disciple. You are someone who does not flinch from the truth.'

Chandogya Upanishad 4:4.1—5

Knowing the unknown

When his son reached the age of twelve, Aruni, who was a priest, said to him: 'It is time for you to go to a spiritual teacher, and become his disciple. Every member of our family studies spiritual knowledge.' So the son went away for twelve years. During this time he learnt all the Vedas, and he returned home at the age of twenty-four.

His father said to him: 'You seem to be very proud of all the knowledge you have acquired. But did you ask your teacher for that wisdom which enables you to hear the unheard, think the unthought, and know the unknown?' The son said: 'What is that wisdom?' Aruni replied: 'By knowing one lump of clay, we come to know all things made out of clay; and we realize that in essence they are the same, differing only in name and form. By knowing one gold nugget, we come to know all things made out of gold; and we realize that in essence they are the same, differing only in name and form. By knowing one tool of iron, we come to know all tools made out of iron; and we realize that in essence they are the same, differing only in name and form. In the same way, through spiritual wisdom we come to know that all life is one.'

The son exclaimed: 'My teacher must have been ignorant of this wisdom; if he had known it, he would surely have taught it to me. Please instruct me.'

Chandogya Upanishad 6:1.1−7

Sleeping in the soul

Aruni spoke: 'In the beginning there was a single soul – one soul, without any others. Out of the soul came the entire universe, and everything that exists within it. There is nothing in the universe that does not come from the soul. The soul dwells within all that exists; it is the truth of all that exists. You, my son, are the soul.'

His son said: 'Father, tell me more about the soul.' Aruni continued: 'Let us start with sleep. What happens when you sleep? When you sink into dreamless sleep, you are in union with the soul – even though you are not aware of this. Think of a bird tethered with string. It flies in all directions; and finally, when it cannot find a resting-place anywhere else, it settles down on the perch to which it is tied. Similarly the mind is tethered to the soul. It flies off in all directions during the day; and at night it settles down within the soul. The soul is the home of all living beings; and from the soul all living beings derive their strength.

'Let us now consider death. When a person dies, speech is absorbed by the mind; the mind is absorbed by the breath; the breath is absorbed by fire; and fire is absorbed within the soul. As I say, there is nothing in the universe that does not come from the soul. The soul dwells within all that exists; it is the truth of all that exists. You, my son, are the soul.' 'Tell me more about the soul,' his son said.

Chandogya Upanishad 6:2.2–3; 8.1–2, 4, 6–7

Bees, rivers and trees

Aruni continued: 'Bees suck nectar from many different flowers, and then make honey. One drop of honey cannot claim to come from one flower, and another drop of honey from another flower; the honey is a single consistent whole. In the same way, all beings are one – even though they are not aware of this. The tiger and the lion, the wolf and the boar, the worm and the moth, the gnat and the mosquito, all come from the soul, and are part of the soul.' 'Tell me more about the soul,' his son said.

Aruni continued: 'Rivers flowing east and rivers flowing west all flow into the sea; and their waters merge with the waters of the sea. One drop of the sea cannot claim to come from one river, and another drop of the sea from another river; the sea is a single consistent whole. In the same way all beings are one; there is no being that does not come from the soul, and is not part of the soul.' 'Tell me more about the soul,' his son said.

Aruni continued: 'Hack at the root of a tree, and its sap will flow; hack at the middle of a tree, and its sap will flow; hack at the top of the tree and its sap will flow. The sap supports and nourishes the tree. In the same way the soul supports and nourishes all that exists. If the sap were to leave a branch of a tree, the branch would die; if it were to leave the whole tree, the tree would die. In the same way, when the soul leaves any being, that being dies – but the soul itself never dies.' 'Tell me more about the soul,' his son said.

Chandogya 6:9.1–3; 10.1–3; 11.1–3

The seed and the blindfold

'Bring me a banyan fruit,' Aruni said; and his son brought him one. 'Cut it in two,' Aruni said; and his son cut it in two. 'What do you see?' Aruni asked. 'I see some very small seeds,' his son replied. 'Take one of the seeds, and cut it in two,' Aruni said; and his son cut a seed in two. 'What do you see?' Aruni asked. 'Nothing at all,' his son replied.

Aruni said: 'Within that seed is the essence which makes the entire tree grow – yet it cannot be seen. In the same way the soul is the essence which gives life to every being in the universe – yet it cannot be seen.' 'Tell me more about the soul,' his son said.

Aruni said: 'A man was once blindfolded, taken far away from his village, and abandoned. The man wandered to the east and west, to the north and south, but he had no idea which way he was going. He called out for help. Eventually someone heard his call, and took off the blindfold. The man now went from one village to another, asking directions, and he found his way back home. In the same way a good teacher takes the blindfold from the spiritual eyes of his pupils. Then they are able to find their way to the soul – which is their true home.' 'Tell me more about the soul,' his son said.

Chandogya Upanishad 6: 12. 1–3; 14. 1–3

The heated blade

Aruni continued: 'It is said that the people of a certain town had an infallible method of judging those accused of crime. They heated the blade of an axe until it was red-hot. Then they asked the accused man whether he was guilty of the crime or not. When he pleaded that he was not guilty, they ordered him to take hold of the blade. If he were guilty of the crime, his hands would be burnt by the heat of the axe; so they would execute him. If he were innocent of the crime, his hands would remain unhurt; so they would release him. The explanation for this method is this. The guilty man, by pleading that he was not guilty, was covering himself with falsehood; and falsehood offers no protection from heat. The innocent man, by contrast, was covering himself with truth; and truth offers perfect protection.'

Aruni concluded: 'Truth is the soul; from the soul comes the universe and all that exists within it – including you, dear son.' Thus Aruni's son learnt about the soul.

Chandogya Upanishad 6:16.1–3

Name, speech and mind

A young man came to the sage Sanatkumara, and asked the
sage to teach him. Sanatkumara replied: 'Tell me what you
already know; and I shall teach what is beyond that.' The
young man said: 'I know the Vedas. I have studied grammar,
mathematics, astronomy, logic, politics, the fine arts, and
even snake charming. But all this knowledge has not helped
me to understand the soul. I have heard that understanding
the soul is the cure for all sorrow. At present I am utterly
miserable.'

Sanatkumara said: 'You know the names of many things.
All these things come from God; and through God all misery
is dispelled. Therefore you should venerate God as name.'

'Is there anything greater than names?' the young man
asked. Sanatkumara replied: 'Speech is greater than names. If
there were no speech, right and wrong could not be made
known, and truth and falsehood could not be distinguished.
Speech is the means of proclaiming right and wrong, and distinguishing truth from falsehood. Therefore you should venerate God as speech.'

'Is there anything greater than speech?' the young man
asked. Sanatkumara replied: 'The mind is greater than speech.
Through the mind you can decide what rituals to perform,
what work to do, and what aims to pursue. Therefore you
should venerate God as mind.'

Chandogya Upanishad 7:1.1−5; 2.1−2; 3.1−2

Intention, thought and meditation

'Is there anything greater than mind?' the young man asked. Sanatkumara replied: 'Intention is greater than mind. In order to make up your mind, you must first form an intention; and having made up your mind, you can express your intention in speech. Thus intention is the point at which mind and speech converge. The earth and sky were fashioned through God's intention; wind and space, water and fire, were also fashioned through God's intention. Indeed, the design of the universe as a whole reveals God's intention. Therefore you should venerate God as intention.'

'Is there anything greater than intention?' the young man asked. Sanatkumara replied: 'Thought is greater than intention. Through thought you can remain constant and steadfast. If you direct your thought to some goal, you can attain that goal. Thought can move with complete freedom. Therefore you should venerate God as thought.'

'Is there anything greater than thought?' the young man asked. Sanatkumara replied: 'Meditation is greater than thought. Through meditation the earth can be understood; through meditation the sky can be understood; through meditation the space between the earth and the sky can be understood. Those who are respected as wise and learned, broad-minded and tolerant, have attained these qualities through meditation. Those who remain foolish and ignorant, small-minded and intolerant, have not meditated. Therefore you should venerate God as meditation.'

Chandogya Upanishad 7:4. 1–3; 5. 1–2; 6. 1–3

From truth to action

Sanatkumara continued: 'When you speak the truth, you utter words of greatness. So you must understand the nature of truth.' The young man said: 'I seek the nature of truth.'

Sanatkumara said: 'When you perceive, you can speak the truth. Those who do not perceive, cannot speak the truth. So you must understand the nature of perception.' The young man said: 'I seek the nature of perception.'

Sanatkumara said: 'When you think, then you can perceive. Those who do not think, cannot perceive. So you must understand the nature of thought.' The young man said: 'I seek the nature of thought.'

Sanatkumara said: 'When you have faith, you can think. Those who do not have faith, cannot think. Therefore you must understand the nature of faith.' The young man said: 'I seek the nature of faith.'

Sanatkumara said: 'When you do good, you can have faith. Those who do no good, cannot have faith. Therefore you must understand the nature of goodness.' The young man said: 'I seek the nature of goodness.'

Sanatkumara said: 'When you act effectively, you can do good. Those who do not act effectively, cannot do good. Therefore you must understand the nature of effective action.' The young man said: 'I seek the nature of effective action.'

Chandogya Upanishad 7:16; 17; 18; 19; 20

From action to infinity

Sanatkumara said: 'When you attain well-being, then you can act effectively. Those who do not attain well-being, cannot act effectively. Therefore you must understand the nature of well-being.' The young man said: 'I seek the nature of well-being.'

Sanatkumara said: 'When you enjoy the beauty of the world, then you can attain well-being. Those who do not enjoy the beauty of the world, cannot attain well-being. Therefore you must understand the nature of beauty.' The young man said: 'I seek the nature of beauty.'

Sanatkumara said: 'When you can discern the infinite in that which is beautiful, then you can enjoy beauty. Those who do not discern the infinite in that which is beautiful, cannot enjoy beauty. Therefore you must understand the infinite.' The young man said: 'I seek the nature of infinity.'

Sanatkumara said: 'When you understand the indivisible unity of all beings, and see and hear nothing, you discern the infinite. When you see or hear only separateness and division, you discern only that which is finite. The infinite is beyond death, but the finite cannot escape death.'

Chandogya Upanishad 7:21; 22; 23; 24.1a

The glory of the infinite

The young man asked: 'On what does the infinite depend?' Sanatkumara replied: 'On its own glory – but not glory in the way the world understands glory. In the world glory is defined by the possession of cattle and horses, elephants and gold, servants and wives, lands and houses. But that is not true glory, because they all depend on each other. The infinite is utterly independent.'

Sanatkumara continued: 'The infinite is above and below; it is the north and the south, the east and the west; the infinite is the whole universe. I am above and below; I am the north and the south, the east and the west; I am the whole universe. The soul is above and below; the soul is the north and the south, the east and the west; the soul is the whole universe. Those who see, know and understand this – and who find in the soul all love and joy – are utterly free. But those who do not understand this – and who pursue the finite – are in spiritual chains.'

Chandogya Upanishad 7:24. 1b–2; 25. 1–2

The perfect light

Sanatkumara continued: 'Those who contemplate the soul, and thereby come to understand the soul, discover that everything in the universe – energy and space, fire and water, name and form, birth and death, mind and intention, word and action, prayer and meditation – comes from the soul.

'The soul is one, though it appears to be many. Those who contemplate the soul, and thereby come to understand the soul, go beyond decay and death, beyond conflict and sorrow. They discern the soul in all beings, and so are in union with all beings.

'Control the senses, and purify the mind. In a pure mind there is constant awareness of the soul. Where there is constant awareness of the soul, bondage is overwhelmed by freedom, and misery is vanquished by joy.'

Thus Sanatkumara taught the young man to transcend the darkness of bondage and misery, and enter the perfect light of the soul.

Chandogya Upanishad 7:26.1–2

The city of God

In the city of God there is a small lotus; and in this lotus there is a tiny dwelling. Within this dwelling is a space; and within that space is the fulfilment of our desires. That which is within that space, should be sought and found.

The tiny space within the lotus is as vast as the space which contains the earth and the sky, the sun and the moon. Everything that is contained within the space around us, is also in the tiny space within the lotus.

Do not be anxious that old age will invade the city of God; do not be anxious that death will ever invade. Within the lotus, which is found in the city of God, all desires are eternally fulfilled. Time does not pass in the city of God, so the body cannot grow old and die – and the body cannot feel hunger or thirst.

In the city of God the soul is supreme. The soul only desires what is real, and it only thinks what is true.

Chandogya Upanishad 8:1.1, 3, 5

The soul as a bridge

The soul is the bridge by which people may pass from mortality to immortality, from the world to the city of God. Day and night cannot cross that bridge; nor can old age, death and grief; nor can good and evil deeds.

Those who are blind as they approach the bridge, have their eyes opened as they cross it. Those who are wounded as they approach the bridge, have their wounds healed as they cross it. Those who are sick as they approach the bridge, are made well as they cross it. Those who are sad as they approach the bridge, become happy as they cross it.

The bridge is the boundary between darkness and light, between the darkness of the world, and the supreme light of God. Darkness can never enter the city of God.

Only those who are pure and self-controlled can cross this bridge into the city of God. The city of God belongs to them, and to them alone. In the city of God they enjoy perfect freedom.

Chandogya Upanishad 8:4.1–3

Reflections in a bowl

The angels once said to one another: 'Let us try to discover the soul, so that we may fulfil all our desires.' So they sent one of their number to the sage Prajapati, carrying fuel in his hands as a sign that he wanted to become a disciple. At the same time the demons said to one another: 'Let us try to discover the soul, so that we may fulfil all our desires.' So they also sent one of their number to the sage Prajapati, carrying fuel in his hands as a sign that he wanted to become a disciple.

The angel and the demon lived with Prajapati for thirty-two years. At the end of that time Prajapati asked why they had stayed with him for so long. They replied: 'We have lived here for all these years because we wish to know the soul.'

Prajapati said to them: 'When you look into the eyes of another being, you see the soul – fearless and immortal. That is God, who is supreme.' The disciples asked: 'When we look at our reflections in the water or in a mirror, what do we see?' Prajapati answered: 'You see the soul.' He instructed them to fill a bowl with water, and look at their reflection within it. 'What do you see in the water?' he asked. They replied: 'We see ourselves, from our hair down to the nails on our feet.' Prajapati said: 'You are seeing the soul – fearless and immortal.'

The angel and demon were satisfied, and left Prajapati.

Chandogya Upanishad 8:7.2–4; 8.1–3

The realm of dreams

When the angel and the demon had left, Prajapati thought: 'They have seen the soul, but they have not recognized the soul. They mistake the body for the soul. Those who think that the body is the soul, will lose themselves.'

The demon remained quite certain that the body is the soul. He returned to the other demons, and told them that the body alone should be adored. He taught them that those who indulge the body's senses, will find joy in this life and the next.

But the angel, as he journeyed home to the other angels, began to have doubts. He thought: 'The notion that the soul is the same as the body, cannot be correct. The soul would be blind when the body were blind; the soul would be lame when the body were lame; the soul would be paralyzed when the body were paralyzed; and when the body died, the soul would die also. That is nonsense.' So he returned to Prajapati, carrying fuel in his hands to indicate that he again wanted to be his disciple.

'Why have you returned?' Prajapati asked. The angel expressed his doubts. Prajapati said: 'Your thoughts are very clear. Live with me for another thirty-two years, and I shall teach you more about the soul.' The angel did so. At the end of that time Prajapati said: 'That which wanders joyfully through the realm of dreams, is the soul – fearless and immortal. And the soul is God, who is supreme.'

The angel was satisfied, and left Prajapati.

Chandogya Upanishad 8:8.4–5; 9.1–3; 10.1a

Dreamless sleep

As he journeyed back to the other angels, the angel began to have doubts. He thought: 'In dreams the soul may appear to suffer or be killed; it may experience pain and grief. So the soul cannot be that which wanders joyfully through the realm of dreams.' The angel returned to Prajapati, and lived with him for another thirty-two years. At the end of that time Prajapati said: 'That which enables a person to sleep soundly, with a tranquil mind undisturbed by dreams, is the soul – fearless and immortal. And the soul is God, who is supreme.' The angel was satisfied, and left Prajapati.

But as he journeyed back to the other angels, the angel began to have doubts. He thought: 'During dreamless sleep you are not aware of yourself, or of any other being. Thus the state of dreamless sleep is very close to extinction. So the soul cannot be that which enables a person to sleep soundly, undisturbed by dreams.' The angel returned to Prajapati, and lived with him for another five years. At the end of that time Prajapati said: 'The body is perishable, but the soul is imperishable. The body is subject to pleasure and pain; no one who identifies with the body, can escape from pleasure and pain. But those who know they are not the body, transcend pleasure and pain, and enjoy perpetual bliss.'

Chandogya Upanishad 8:10.1b–4; 11.1–3; 12.1

The transcendent light

Prajapati continued: 'The wind does not have a body, nor does lightning, nor does thunder, nor do clouds; they rise through space without physical shape, and reach the transcendent light. In the same way human beings who rise above awareness of the body, reach the transcendent light. Wind, lightning, thunder and clouds have forms which are not physical. Human beings who rise above awareness of the body, take a form which is not physical; it is the form of the soul.

'In this form human beings are free from all attachments. They move wherever they want, and laugh whenever they want. They know that the soul is only tied to the body for a short time, as an ox is tied to its cart. Whenever they see, it is the soul seeing; whenever they speak, it is the soul speaking; whenever they hear, it is the soul hearing; and whenever they think, it is the soul thinking. The senses are merely their instruments, to use as they choose.

'When the angels surrounding God worship and adore the soul, they are filled with joy; all their desires are satisfied. Equally when human beings on earth seek and know the soul, they are filled with joy, and all their desires are satisfied.'

Chandogya Upanishad 8:12.2

Understanding connections

May the God of day grant us peace. May the God of night grant us peace. May the God of sight grant us peace. May the God of strength grant us peace. May the God of speech grant us peace. May the God of space grant us peace.

I bow down to God, the source of all power. I speak the truth, and obey his commandments. May God guard me and my teacher against all harm. May the glory of sacred knowledge illumine us, and may God unite us to himself.

We contemplate five things: the world; light; education; progeny; and speech. What is the world? It is the earth below and the sky above – and the air in space that connects them. What is light? It is fire below and the sun above – and the lightning that connects them. What is education? It is the teacher above and the disciple below – and the wisdom that connects them. What is progeny? It is the father above and the mother below – and the sexual organ that connects them. What is speech? It is the upper jaw and the lower jaw – and the tongue that connects them. Those who understand these connections, will be richly blessed.

Taittiriya Upanishad I:I; 3. I–6

Spiritual ambitions

God, revealed in sacred texts, has assumed the forms of all creatures. May he grant me wisdom to choose the path which leads to immortality. May my body be healthy, and my tongue be sweet. May my ears always hear the sound of Aum, the supreme symbol of God. And may love for God grow stronger and stronger.

May I deepen in spiritual wisdom, and also have ample food to eat and clothes to wear. May disciples flock to me from near and far. May I show them how to control their senses and calm their minds; success as a spiritual teacher is the wealth and the fame which I crave.

May I enter God; and may God enter me. Through God I shall be cleansed and made pure.

As a river flows down the mountain, may disciples flow towards me. As days accumulate into months and years, may disciples accumulate around me. May disciples come to me from every land in the world.

God is my neighbour. He will always shine upon me.

Taittiriya Upanishad 1:4.1–3

Sacred sounds

Bhur, bhuvas, and suvar are three sacred sounds. Maha is a fourth sacred sound, which represents the soul; the other three sounds represent the limbs of the soul.

Bhur may be regarded as the earth, bhuvas as space above the earth, and suvar as the sky at the top of space. Then maha is the sun that sustains all life, and is a source of joy.

Bhur may be regarded as fire, bhuvas as air, and suvar as the sun. Then maha is the moon, which supports all the lights in the sky.

Bhur may be regarded as breathing in, bhuvas as breathing out, and suvar as holding the breath between breathing in and breathing out. Then maha is food, which sustains all life, and is a source of joy.

Those who understand these sacred sounds, know the soul – and are respected by all beings.

Taittiriya Upanishad 1:5. 1–2, 4–5

Unity through chanting

God dwells in the hearts of all beings. If you know God, you transcend death. God may be found between the two halves of the palate, and between the two halves of the skull.

When you chant bhur, you are unified with fire. When you chant bhuvas, you are unified with air. When you chant suvar, you are unified with the sun. And when you chant maha, you are unified with God.

By this chanting, you become master of yourself; you rule over your emotions, your senses, and your mind. By this chanting you know truth, you experience peace, and you attain immortality. By this chanting you reach the source of all joy, and you realize the supreme goal of all existence. By this chanting you meditate on God, the source of all of life. Meditate always on him.

Taittiriya Upanishad 1:6.1–2

The holiness of all things

Consider the world in which we live. There is the earth above, the sky below, and the space between them. Each may be divided into four quarters; and each quarter may be divided into two halves. There is fire, water and air; there is the sun, the moon and the stars; and there are plants and trees.

Consider the human body. There are eyes and ears; there is the mind and the tongue; there is skin, through which the sense of touch operates; there is flesh and muscle; there are bones, and the marrow of bones; there is breathing out, breathing in, and holding the breath between breathing in and breathing out.

If you contemplate the world and the human body, you discover that all things are holy. Through contemplation you understand the unity between the outer existence of the world and the body, and the inner existence of the soul.

Taittiriya Upanishad 1:7

Aum as the divine symbol

Aum is the supreme symbol of God. Aum is the whole. Aum
affirms. Aum is the sound which expresses all truth.

The priest begins worship with Aum. Spiritual teachers
begin their lessons with Aum; and their disciples open themselves to those lessons with Aum.

Those in whom Aum resides, are unified with God.

Taittiriya Upanishad 1:8

Living in the world

Do you live and work in the world? Always act according to the highest moral standards, both in private and in public. Always be honest in word and deed, both in private and in public. Master your emotions and control your senses, both in private and in public. Be calm and patient, both in private and in public. Worship with sincere devotion, both in private and in public. Take every opportunity to serve others, both in private and in public. Be kind and gentle to your children, both in private and in public.

Yes, always act according to the highest moral standards; and always be honest in word and deed. And be the same in private and in public. All this is necessary if you are to make spiritual progress.

Taittiriya Upanishad 1:9

The tree of life

'I have become one with the tree of life. My glory rises as high as the highest mountain peak. I have come to know and understand the soul – which is totally pure and wise, and which shines with the perfect radiance of immortality.' Thus speaks the wise teacher who is unified with God.

The wise teacher continues: 'Speak honestly, and act rightly. Do not neglect to recite the Vedas. Uphold the customs of your family. Do not deviate from that which is true and good. When you have moved forward in spiritual understanding, do not allow yourself to slide backwards. Learn from those who are wiser than you, and teach those who are less wise. Treat all wise teachers with respect. Look for that which is divine in your mother and your father, in friends and in strangers. Honour those who are worthy of honour.

'Give with faith, and never without faith. Give with dignity. Give with humility. Give with joy. And give with understanding of the effects of your gift.

'If you are ever in doubt as to how to behave, seek the advice of someone wiser than yourself; there are always people with experience and shrewdness who can guide you. If you follow good advice, you can be sure of making spiritual progress.'

Taittiriya Upanishad 1:10; 11

Proclaiming and thanking God

May God be kind to us. We worship God as the Creator. We worship God as the soul. We worship God the sustainer of all that is visible.

I proclaim God. I proclaim his presence in all living beings. I proclaim him as goodness and righteousness. I proclaim him as truth and wisdom.

I thank God. I thank him for his help. I thank him for his guidance. I thank him for the teacher he has given me. I thank him for helping and guiding my teacher.

Aum! Peace! Peace! Peace!

Taittiriya Upanishad 1:12

Food and air

Truth and knowledge are hidden in the deepest cave; they are hidden above the highest cloud. Those who know this, have all their desires fulfilled.

From the soul space came into existence; from space air came into existence; from air, fire; from fire, water; from water, earth; from earth, plants; from plants, food; and from food, the human body – the head, the arms, the legs, and the heart.

From food all bodies are made; and after death each body becomes food for others. Food is vital to the body; therefore the right food is the best medicine for the body's ailments. Those who look upon food as a gift from God, will enjoy good health.

Men and women, animals and birds, need to breathe air; breathing air is the source of life itself. Air is vital to the body, determining how long the body lives. Those who look upon air as a gift from God, will complete the full span of life.

Taittiriya Upanishad 2:1; 2; 3

The mind and wisdom

When words try to approach God, they are forced to turn back. Human thought can never reach God. Yet human beings can know the bliss of God, and thereby be freed from all fear.

The mind is like a body. Thought is its skin, faith its head, righteousness its right arm, and truth its left. The practice of meditation is its heart, and discernment its feet.

Wisdom is like a body, contained within the mind. Bliss is its skin, joy its head, contentment its right arm, and delight its left. Selfless service is its heart, and spiritual understanding its feet.

Even the angels seek wisdom. Human beings can attain perfect wisdom, and thereby be free from all sin.

Taittiriya Upanishad 2:5

The incarnate God

Those who deny God, deny themselves. Those who affirm God, affirm themselves.

God said: 'Let me multiply! Let me have offspring!' So he heated himself up; and when he was hot, he emitted the entire world, and all that it contains. And after emitting the world, he entered it. He who has no body, assumed many bodies. He who is infinite, became finite. He who is everywhere, went to particular places. He who is totally wise, caused ignorance. He who sees all truth, caused delusion. God becomes every being, and gives reality to every being.

Before the world was created, God existed, but was invisible. By means of the soul all living beings can know God; and this knowledge fills them with joy. The soul is the source of abiding joy. When we discover the soul in the depths of our consciousness, we are overwhelmed with delight. If the soul did not live within us, then we should not breathe – we should not live.

The soul is one. The soul is changeless, nameless, and formless. Until we understand the soul, we live in fear. Scholars may study the soul through words; but unless they know the soul within themselves, their scholarship merely emphasizes their ignorance, and increases their fear.

Taittiriya Upanishad 2:6; 7

A hundred measures of joy

Awe of God makes the wind blow. Awe of God makes the sun shine. Awe of God makes fire burn. And awe of God makes rain fall.

Consider a young man. He is healthy and strong, learned and intelligent. He possesses as much wealth as the world can provide. Thus we may say that he has one measure of joy. If he were to be free from all attachments, he would have a hundred measures of joy.

The soul within us and the sun are one. Those who understand this, see the world as it really is; and they understand the unity of all life. They do not agonize about right and wrong. They do not ask themselves: 'Why did I not do the right thing?' Nor do they ask themselves: 'Why did I do the wrong thing?' Those who know the soul, are not oppressed by these two questions. And those who are not oppressed by these two questions, are utterly free. They know the joy of God; so they transcend the duality of right and wrong.

Taittiriya Upanishad 2:8; 9

From food to bliss

A young man called Bhrigu went to his father, Varuna, and asked: 'What is God?' Varuna replied: 'First strive to understand food, breath, sight, hearing, mind, and speech. Then strive to know that from which these things are born, by which they are sustained, for which they search, and to which they return. That is God.'

Bhrigu meditated. After a time he thought: 'Food is God – for food is that from which things are born, by which they are sustained, for which they search, and to which they return.'

Bhrigu meditated again. After a time he thought: 'Breath is God – for breath is that from which things are born, by which they are sustained, for which they search, and to which they return.'

Bhrigu meditated again. After a time he thought: 'Mind is God – for mind is that from which things are born, by which they are sustained, for which they search, and to which they return.'

Bhrigu meditated again. After a time he thought: 'Wisdom is God – for wisdom is that from which things are born, by which they are sustained, for which they search, and to which they return.'

Bhrigu meditated again. After a time he thought: 'Bliss is God – for bliss is that from which things are born, by which they are sustained, for which they search, and to which they return.'

Taittiriya Upanishad 3:1; 2; 3; 4; 5; 6

Food and the soul

Respect food, for food sustains the body; and the body exists to serve the soul.

Do not waste food; do not waste water; and do not waste fire. Fire and water exist to serve the soul.

Grow much food. The earth can yield as much food as people want – and more. Earth exists to serve the soul.

Do not turn away the poor and the hungry, but feed them freely. When you feed the hungry, you serve God, who created all living beings.

Those who are aware of the soul within the body, possess great strength, and will flourish in this life. Their relatives and their neighbours love and respect them. Their words are always pleasing to those who listen. Their arms are always willing to serve others. Their feet are always ready to go to the help of the needy.

Look for God within every animal and bird, and in the light of every star. Look for God in sexual intercourse, and in the rain that falls from the sky. Look for God in everything that the world contains. Look for God within yourself; and through him destroy all that is evil in your heart and mind.

Taittiriya Upanishad 3:7; 8; 9; 10. 1–4

Three births in a human life

A human life begins as sexual fluid, which has been gathered in the father's sexual organ from his entire body. When this fluid is passed to the mother, it becomes a child. The formation of the child within the mother is the first birth. Child and mother are one. She carries the child in her womb, and protects it. The father loves the child, even while it is in the womb. The child is the soul of the mother and father. The emergence of the child from the mother's womb is the second birth. In taking care of the infant, the mother and father are taking care of themselves. The infant grows into an adult, and then grows old. Death is the third birth, because after death the person is born again.

A sage once said: 'I recall dwelling in my mother's womb. The womb is as strong as a hundred fortresses made of iron. But I broke free, emerging into the world like a falcon flying from a cage.'

Aitareya Upanishad 2:1.1—5

The greatest gift

A man came to God's house. God said to him: 'Ask for a gift.'
The man replied: 'I ask for that gift which you think is most
beneficial for a human being.' God replied: 'I cannot impose
a gift on a being who is inferior to me. You must choose a
gift for yourself.' The man said: 'Then I shall not have a gift.'

But God did not leave the path of truth, because he is
truth. He thus said to the man: 'Look upon me, and know
me. To know me is the greatest gift that a human being can
have. When people know me, nothing – not even their own
sins – can truly harm them.'

God continued: 'I am the breath of life, and the consciousness of life. Worship me as life and immortality. When
you speak, let life speak; when you see,
let life see; when you hear, let life hear;
when you think, let life think; when
you breathe, let life breathe.'

Kaushitaki Upanishad 3:1; 2

The sense of the senses

A young man asked his spiritual teacher: 'What makes my mind think? What gives my body vitality? What causes my tongue to speak? What sees through my eyes and hears through my ears?'

The teacher replied: 'The soul is the sense of the senses. It is the ear of the ear, the eye of the eye, the mind of the mind, the speech of speech, and the life of life. Yet our eyes cannot see the soul; our tongues cannot describe the soul; and our minds cannot analyze the soul. The soul is different from all that can be perceived by the senses.

'The soul is that which causes the tongue to speak, yet cannot be spoken by the tongue. The soul is that which makes the mind think, yet cannot be thought by the mind. The soul is that which sees through the eyes, yet cannot be seen by the eyes. The soul is that which hears through the ears, yet cannot be heard by the ears. The soul is that which induces breathing, yet cannot be inhaled or exhaled. The soul is you, and is not something other than you.'

Kena Upanishad 1.1–8

Knowing the soul

The teacher said: 'You may think that you already know the soul. At present you are only aware of the outward manifestations of the soul; you do not know the soul in itself.' The young man replied: 'I do not think I know the soul. My ignorance is such that I cannot even say that I do not know the soul.'

The teacher said: 'There is only one way of knowing the soul: to know the soul within yourself. The ignorant think they can know the soul through the senses. But all knowledge through the senses involves the duality of the knower and the known. Knowledge of the soul transcends the duality of the knower and the known; it unifies the subject and the object.

'Thus to know the soul within yourself you must rise to a higher level of consciousness. At this higher level you no longer identify yourself with your body; and so physical birth and death cease to matter – you are immortal.

'To know the soul is to dwell in perfect light. To be ignorant of the soul is to dwell in utter darkness. Thus knowledge of the soul within yourself should be the only goal of your life.'

Kena Upanishad 2. 1–5

The paths of joy and pleasure

There is a path of joy, and there is a path of pleasure. The soul is attracted to both paths. Those who follow the path of joy, reach a destination at which joy is complete. Those who follow the path of pleasure, never reach a destination. These two paths lie in front of us. The wise person chooses the path of joy; the ignorant person chooses the path of pleasure.

There are many ignorant people who imagine themselves to be wise and learned. They lead others, without knowing where they are going; they are the blind leading the blind.

The path of joy is invisible to those who never meditate, and who are deluded by pleasure. They say: 'The life we lead, is the only life; and the world we inhabit, is the only world.' Thus they go from one death to another.

Not many people follow the path of joy; and even fewer reach the end. Those who have followed this path, and can teach others how to follow it, are spiritual heroes. Those who want to follow this path, and wish to be taught, are also spiritual heroes.

You cannot follow the path of joy through logic and reason. You need a teacher in whom you can place complete trust.

Katha Upanishad 2.1–2, 5–9

Beyond cause and effect

There is a single word that expresses all truth and contains all worship. The word is Aum. This word is the eternal God; it is the highest glory. When you know that word, all your desires are fulfilled. It is the supreme means of salvation; it is the supreme source of help. When that word reverberates within you, then you know the soul.

The soul was never born, nor will it die. The soul is beyond cause and effect; it is eternal and immutable. When the body dies, the soul does not die. If you believe you can slay another person, or be slain by another person, you are deluded; the soul, the true self, can never be slain.

The soul is hidden in the heart of every living being. It is smaller than the smallest grain, and greater than the entire universe. If you behold the glory of the soul, all sorrow will be dispelled, and all selfish cravings will be extinguished. When you are meditating, the soul guides your meditation; and when you rise from meditation, the soul guides your movements. You can never escape from the soul.

The soul is that which is formless amidst forms, that which is changeless amidst change. The soul is everywhere at once. The soul cannot be known through scholarship, nor through reason, nor through debate. The soul can only be known by those to whom the soul reveals itself. And the soul will never reveal itself to those who fail to act righteously, who fail to control the mind and the senses, and who do not meditate.

Katha Upanishad 2.15–24

The body as a chariot

Think of the soul as the master of a chariot. The body is the chariot itself, the faculty of reason is the rider, and the mind is the reins. The senses are the horses, and desires are the roads on which they travel.

When the master of a chariot has full control of the chariot, the rider, the reins and the horses, then the chariot moves swiftly and smoothly. In the same way when the soul controls the body, the mind and the senses, life is joyful and happy. But when the master lacks control, the horses run wild. In the same way when the body, the mind and the senses are not controlled by the soul, there is misery and pain.

The objects of desire guide the senses. The senses supply information to the mind, and so influence what the mind thinks. The thoughts of the mind are ordered by the faculty of reason. And reason only operates successfully when it is guided by the soul. Reason and the mind can be trained to hear the guidance of the soul, and obey it. This training takes the form of meditation, by which reason and the mind rise to a higher level of consciousness.

So wake up, rise to your feet, and seek a teacher who can train you.

Katha Upanishad 3.3–7, 10–14

Turning the senses inward

When God created human beings, he fashioned the senses to perceive external objects and events. But wise people turn the senses inward, in order to perceive the soul.

Foolish people chase outward pleasures; and so they fall into the snare of death. Wise people know that outward pleasures are fleeting, so they ignore them; they want only that joy which is eternal.

Foolish people are enthralled by bright clothes and happy songs, by sweet perfumes and loving kisses. Wise people are concerned only with what lies behind all these things. Just as bees fly from one blossom to another, looking only for the essence of each one, wise people look only for the essence of every person they meet.

Wise people, who know and understand the soul, are indifferent to both pleasure and pain; they have risen above sensations. They are indifferent to the past and the future; they have risen above time. They are indifferent to danger; they have risen above fear.

Wise people know that what is here, is also there; that what was, will also be. They see unity, not division.

Katha Upanishad 4.1—5, 10—11

The supremacy of the soul

The soul is the sun shining in the sky. It is the wind blowing in space. It is the fire warming the home on a cold night. The soul dwells amongst the stars in the sky, and within every living being. It dwells in the fish swimming in the sea, in the plant growing on the earth, and in the river flowing down the mountain. The soul is supreme.

The powers of life worship the soul. It rules every breath. All the senses pay homage. When the soul breaks the bonds which tie it to a body, then the body dies. The soul is supreme. We live not by the breath that flows in and out of our lungs, but by that which causes the breath to flow – the soul.

After death the soul may go into the womb of a mother, and so obtain a new body. The soul may go into a tree or a plant. The destination of the soul after death depends on the quality of the previous life – on how much wisdom was acquired, and how many good works were performed.

The soul is awake even when we are asleep; the soul creates our dreams, giving form to our deepest desires.

The soul is God. Every world in the universe depends on the soul; and beyond the soul no world can go. The soul is supreme.

Katha Upanishad 5.2–8

The shape of the soul

A fire assumes different shapes, according to the objects it is consuming. Air assumes different shapes, according to the places it enters. In the same way the soul takes the shape of every being in whom it is present.

The sun cannot be tainted by the defects in the eyes that look at it, or by the defects in the objects on which it shines. In the same way the soul cannot be tainted by the suffering of the world, or by the evils of the beings in whom it dwells.

The soul, which is one, multiplies into many, in order to inhabit the many living beings in the world. Those who discern the soul within their hearts, enjoy eternal bliss; there is no other means of enjoying eternal bliss except through discerning the soul.

The soul is changeless, amidst constant change. The soul is pure consciousness within all who are conscious. The soul, which is one, answers the many prayers of all living beings.

The sun does not shine by its own light; nor does the moon; nor does any star; nor does lightning; nor does any fire lit on earth. All these things shine by the reflection of the soul. The soul is light; and every light derives from the soul.

Katha Upanishad 5.9−13, 15

The tree of eternity

The tree of eternity has its roots in the sky, and its branches reach down to earth. It is God; it is the immortal soul.

The whole universe comes from God; his energy burns like fire, and his power reverberates like thunder, in every part of the universe. In honour of God the sun shines, the clouds rain, and the winds blow. Death itself goes about its business in fear of God.

If you fail to see God in the present life, then after death you must take on another body; if you see God, then you will break free from the cycle of birth and death. God can be seen, like the reflection in a mirror, in a pure heart.

When the senses are calm and the mind is motionless, then your heart is pure; you have reached the highest state of consciousness, in which you are unified with God. If this state of consciousness is firm and secure, so it can never be broken, then you are free.

To calm the senses and still the mind, you must abandon the self. You must renounce 'I' and 'me' and 'mine'. You must suppress every desire that surges around the heart. You must untie every knot of attachment.

A hundred and one lights radiate from the heart. One of them shines upwards to the crown of the head. This points the way to immortality. Every other light points to death.

Katha Upanishad 6.1–5, 10–11, 13–16

The glory of God

Look around you, and see God's glory in all that lives and moves. Enjoy the glory of God by wanting nothing for yourself. Regard nothing as belonging to you; and envy nothing that belongs to others. When you know in your heart that all things belong to God, then all things will bring you pleasure.

If you possess nothing, then you will become an instrument of God. Your work will be his work. And as an instrument of God, you will be perfectly free.

God himself never moves; yet he is swifter than thought. God is stationary; yet the senses can never perceive him. God is beyond the mind and the senses. God stands still; yet he overtakes even the fastest athlete. God is like a calm lake, and also like a stream flowing down a mountain.

God travels, and yet he does not travel. He is far away, and yet he is near. He is within all beings, and yet he is outside all beings.

Those who find God within themselves, and find God in others, lose all fear. Those who are at one with all beings, and discern the unity of all beings, lose all sorrow.

God is light, and all comes from him. God has no body, and so cannot be hurt. He is pure, and so cannot be tainted by evil. He is both immanent and transcendent; he is below and above; he is everywhere.

Isa Upanishad 1–2, 4–8

Action and meditation

Those for whom only the external world matters, live in a dark night. Those for whom only the internal world is real, live in an even darker night. People in the first group lead a life solely of action; people in the second group lead a life solely of meditation. But those who combine action with meditation, cross the sea of death to the land of immortality.

Those who believe God is only transcendent, live in a dark night. Those who believe that God is only immanent, live in a dark night. People in the first group fail to see the unity of all that exists, and people in the second group fail to see the glory. But those who know that God is both immanent and transcendent, cross the sea of death to the land of immortality.

May earthly life become immortal life, when the body becomes dust and ashes. May every mind meditate on eternal God; and may God lead every living being towards eternal joy.

Isa Upanishad 9–14, 17–18

The wheel of life

Who created the world? Is God the Creator? From where do we come? What power sustains us? Where will we find peace? Who governs the sensations of pleasure and pain which drive our actions?

Did the world come into being because time began? Did the world spring into existence by necessity or by chance? Did separate elements combine to form the world? Is the world a manifestation of energy?

Is every event in the world the effect of a cause? Can the soul transcend the process of cause and effect? Can the soul rise above pleasure and pain?

Through deep contemplation sages can discern the power of God, hidden within his own creation. They affirm that God is the cause of all that exists; God sustains every living being; and God is the ruler of time.

The sages see the world as the wheel of God, turning round and round, with all living beings inhabiting its rim. The energy in the world flows from God at the centre, and back to God.

The sages see life as a wheel, with each individual going round and round through birth and death. Individuals remain on this wheel so long as they believe themselves to be separate; but once they realize their unity with God, then they break free.

Svetasvatara Upanishad 1.1—6

Fire in sticks

God is the eternal reality, and the foundation of all existence. Those who perceive him in every living being, are unified with him, and break free from the wheel of life and death.

God holds the world in his hands. He holds the seen and unseen, the transient and the permanent. Those who regard themselves as separate from God, pursue pleasure, and thereby become slaves to pleasure. But when they see God, they are liberated.

The senses perceive constant change. But God is unchanging. Meditate upon him; be absorbed by him; break the illusion of separateness. When you know God, all chains fall away. When you cease to identify yourself with your body, you transcend the decay and death to which the body is subject.

Enshrine God in your heart. When you know him, there is nothing more to know. Meditate upon him. Then you will realize that the whole world is filled with his presence.

Fire is always present; yet it cannot be seen until the art of rubbing two sticks together is learnt. God is always present; yet he cannot be seen until the art of meditation is learnt.

Like oil in sesame seeds, like butter in cream, like water in springs, and like fire in sticks, God dwells in all things.

Svetasvatara Upanishad 1.7−8, 10−13, 15

Progress in meditation

Let the spirit of God blow within you, that the fire of devotion may burn brightly. Drink deeply in the ocean of God's love, that the soul may be nourished.

Dedicate yourself to God, who created the world. He will remove every cause of suffering, and free you from the consequences of your sins.

Sit upright, with your back as straight as a column. Turn your senses and your mind within. Set the word Aum echoing in your heart. Then you will begin to cross the dreadful sea of birth and death.

Train your senses to obey your commands. Control your conduct, so that every action is directed towards God. Hold the reins of your mind, as you would hold the reins of a restive horse.

For meditation choose a place that is clean, quiet and cool. Look for a cave protected against wind and rain, with a smooth floor free from stones and dust.

When you meditate you may see images like snow or smoke. You may feel a gust of wind or a wave of heat. Lightning may seem to flash. These are signs that you are travelling on the road to God.

Gradually your health will improve, your body will lose weight, your skin will glow, and your voice will become clear and resonant. These show that you are making progress.

Svetasvatara Upanishad 2.6−13

Infinitely small and infinitely large

God cast the net of appearance over the world, producing the shapes and colours we see around us. He existed before the world began; and he will exist after the world has ended. He is immortal; and those who know him, become immortal.

God is one. He rules all living beings from within their hearts. The world came from him at the beginning of time; he sustains the world through the passage of time; and at the end of time he will take the world back into himself.

His eyes, his mouths, his arms, and his feet are everywhere. He holds the world together. He is the source of the powers of life. He pervades everything.

There is nothing higher than God, and there is nothing separate from God. He is infinitely small, and infinitely large. He is the roots of the world, the trunk of the world, and its branches.

God fills the world, and yet he transcends it. Those who know God, transcend sorrow and death. Those who do not know him, remain trapped by suffering.

God wants us to know him. He prompts our hearts to seek him. His flame shines within us, showing us the way to him. By stilling the mind we can find him.

Svetasvatara Upanishad 3.1–4, 7, 9–10, 12

Thousands of heads

God has thousands of heads, thousands of eyes, and thousands of feet. He surrounds the world on every side. He is the world. He is all that has happened in the past, and all that will happen in the future. Yet he never changes.

His hands and feet are everywhere; his heads and mouths are everywhere. He sees everything, and hears everything; he pervades everything. Every eye and every ear of every living being is his; he sees through every eye, and hears through every ear.

He moves through the world assuming countless different forms; he takes the form of every kind of living being, and every kind of inanimate object. And he moves through the world without form – running without feet, holding without hands, seeing without eyes, and hearing without ears.

He is hidden in the heart of every living being. He is smaller than the smallest object, and bigger than the world itself. Through his grace we can shed all selfish desires, and dispel all sorrow – and be united with him.

Svetasvatara Upanishad 3.14–20

The veil of difference

May God, from whom all living beings come, and to whom all will return, grant us the gift of wisdom.

He is fire and the sun; he is the moon and the stars; he is the air and the sea. He is this boy, and that girl; he is this man, and that woman; and he is these old people, leaning on their sticks. He appears in countless different forms.

He is the bird with blue feathers, and the bird with green feathers. He is the cloud from which thunder rolls and lightning flashes. He is the seasons of the year, and the waters that cover the oceans. He has no beginning, and he has no end. He is the source of all things.

From God all types of living being acquire their name and form. He determines what will give them pleasure, and what will cause them pain. Each type of living being is distinct and different. But when we pierce the veil of difference, we see the unity of all beings.

Svetasvatara Upanishad 4.1–5

The source of all religions

What use are sacred texts to those who do not know their source? Studying sacred texts is useless in itself; but by knowing the one who inspired them, human beings enjoy eternal peace.

All sacred texts, all genuine worship, and all sincere prayers come from God. All the world comes from God. Look at what God has made – and enjoy its beauty. Every boy and every girl was fashioned by him; every bird and every animal is the work of his hands. Every morsel of food which they eat, is provided by him. From him every living being draws the breath of life.

God is the ruler of time. The angels and the sages know him; and when a man or a woman comes to know him, he cuts the bonds of death. God is hidden in the heart of every living being, as cream is hidden in milk. Those who know him in their hearts, attain immortality.

God is the source of all religions. He is the ruler of the realm of light, where there is neither night nor day. This realm has no material objects; things neither exist, nor do not exist. It is beyond the reach of the mind, and beyond the sight of the eye. It can only be known in the depths of meditation.

God, in you we seek refuge. In you every man and woman, every cow and horse, seeks protection. Save all living beings from the bondage of death.

Svetasvatara Upanishad 4.8–11, 13–16, 18, 20–22

The spell of pleasure and pain

Both ignorance and knowledge are hidden in the mystery of God. Ignorance passes away, and knowledge is immortal; but God encompasses both.

God is the root and flower of every living being. He laid out the field of life in which every being grows and flourishes. He created the powers of creation. Just as the radiance of the sun shines everywhere, so the glory of God shines on all that he has made.

God makes all living beings blossom and bear fruit. He gives all living beings their fragrance and their colour. He alone rules the world. He is the supreme Creator, to which every sacred text bears witness.

We live under the spell of pleasure and pain; we desire pleasure, and fear pain. We imagine that we control our destiny; yet we wander aimlessly from birth to birth, driven by desire and fear. If we turn inwards to seek the soul, it seems no bigger than the breadth of a hair.

The soul is neither male nor female, nor is it neuter; it takes the gender of the body it inhabits. The soul is born again and again, in body after body; and the desires and fears of each body are the consequences of actions in former lives.

But when a person comes to know the soul in all its greatness and its beauty, then there is freedom.

Svetasvatara Upanishad 5.1–11, 14

Knowing God

Some say that life created itself; others say that life evolved through time. God is the ruler of creation and time; all that exists, comes from him.

God is pure consciousness. He is everywhere; he possesses all power; he sees every event. He created time; and living beings evolve at his command.

Those who act without thought of personal gain, and who control their actions, will eventually discover God; and then they will know that all forms of life are one. Those who work in the service of God, are freed from the process of cause and effect.

Know God as the source of life, whose glory permeates the entire world. Know him as the one who is beyond space and time, and yet can be found within the human heart.

Know God as the one who makes the sun and the moon move across the sky. Know him as the one who determines what is right and wrong, and whose law is written on the human heart.

Know God as the king of all kings, the lord of all lords, the ruler of all. Know him as the one who never moves, and yet who is constantly active in the world.

Know God as the first cause of all things, and yet who himself has no cause. Know him as the Lord of love, who conceals himself in all living beings, as a spider conceals itself in its web.

Svetasvatara Upanishad 6.1–10

The Creator and destroyer

God is the operator, and we are his instruments. He is the giver of happiness, and we are the receivers.

He is that which is still, amidst continuous flux. He is that which is conscious within consciousness. He is the liberator who can set us free.

Neither the sun, nor the moon, nor the stars, nor fire, shine by themselves; they reflect the light of God. And God will shine with even greater brightness on our hearts.

God is the Creator of all that exists; and he is the destroyer of all that exists. He alone can destroy death.

God is our refuge. He is the silence of eternity. He is the beauty of perfection. He is the bridge to immortality. He is the fire which burns up life and death.

Can human beings roll up the sky like a piece of deerskin? Can human beings end their misery without the help of God? Only by worshipping God within the human heart can sorrow end, and bliss begin.

Svetasvatara Upanishad 6.12–14, 16–20

Higher and lower knowledge

What is that by which, when known, all is known?

There are two kinds of knowledge, higher and lower. The study of sacred texts, of religion, of astronomy, and of all the arts, is lower knowledge. Higher knowledge is knowledge of the soul.

The eye cannot see the soul, and the mind cannot grasp it. The soul has no race, and it does not belong to any social class. It has neither eyes, nor ears, nor hands, nor feet. It is vast and tiny; it is eternal and changeless. It is the source of all life.

As the web comes forth from the spider, as plants sprout from the earth, and as hair grows from the body, the universe springs from the soul. The universe is the energy of the soul; and from this energy comes life, consciousness, and the elements. The universe is the will of the soul; and from this will comes the law of cause and effect.

The immortal soul sees all; nothing escapes the soul's gaze. From the soul one became many; but in the soul many are one.

Mundaka Upanishad 1:1.3–9

Crossing the sea

Rituals and sacrifices are expressions of lower knowledge. If you wish to become wise, ignore all rituals and sacrifices, and go in search of higher knowledge. In crossing the sea of birth and death, rituals and sacrifices are like leaking rafts.

Religious people, who devote themselves to rituals and sacrifices, are ignorant of their ignorance. In their own estimation they are wise; and they are proud of their religious learning. Yet they are like fools who walk round and round in circles, going nowhere. They urge others to participate in their rituals and sacrifices. Yet they are like the blind leading the blind. They live in the darkness of spiritual adolescence, unaware of any higher purpose.

But those who practise meditation, and who conquer their senses and passions, purify their hearts, and thereby acquire knowledge of the soul – which is the source of all light and life.

Action motivated by pleasure or profit cannot help anyone cross the sea of birth and death. A teacher is required, who has already navigated the sea himself. But even a teacher is useless, unless the disciple sincerely yearns for truth.

Mundaka Upanishad 1:2.1, 7–13

Sparks from a fire

As sparks fly from a blazing fire, so millions of living beings come from God.

He transcends all beings; yet he is present in all beings. He has no body or mind; yet all bodies and minds were created by him. He has no name or form; yet he is the source of all the elements – space, air, fire, water and earth – from which all forms are made.

Fire is his head. The sun and moon are his eyes. The two halves of the sky are his ears. The wind is his breath, and the entire universe is his heart. The earth is his footstool.

From him comes sunshine and rain, which cause seeds to germinate and to grow. From him comes sexual intercourse, which causes women and female animals to become pregnant, and new life to be born. From him come all sacred texts, all holy chants, and all prayers. From him comes work and time. And from him come all righteous acts.

From him come angels and humans, animals and birds. From him comes the art of meditation and the gift of faith. From him comes a pure heart. From him come the levels of consciousness. From him comes wisdom and immortality.

Mundaka Upanishad 2:1.1–8, 10

Shooting the arrow

Take the bow revealed in the sacred texts, and place upon it an arrow sharpened with devotion. Then with great concentration draw the bowstring, and aim at the target.

The bow is the syllable Aum; the arrow is the heart; the bowstring is meditation; and the target is God. Within the heart lies the soul; and when the arrow hits the target, there is perfect unity.

In God's robe are woven the earth and the sky, and also mind and body. God is dressed in all the powers of life.

The nerves of the body are like the spokes of a wheel; at the hub is the heart. By meditating on the syllable Aum, a person may follow the spokes to the hub.

The heart is like a golden city, with lights shining brightly on every street. And all the streets lead to the centre of the city, which is the soul.

Mundaka Upanishad
2:2.3–6, 10

Two birds

There are two birds, who are intimate friends, perched on the same tree. One bird eats the fruits of the tree, both the sweet fruits and the bitter ones. The other bird silently looks on. The first bird represents those who are attached to the things of this world, and so experience pleasure and pain. The second bird represents those who are detached from the things of this world, and so are free from pleasure and pain.

As long as you pursue pleasure, you are attached to the sources of pleasure; and as long as you are attached to the sources of pleasure, you cannot escape pain and sorrow. But when you stop pursuing pleasure, and find the source of light and love which lies within the heart, then you rise above pleasure and pain, and enjoy eternal bliss.

The soul shines in the hearts of all living beings. When you see the soul in others, you forget your own desires and fears, and lose yourself in the service of others. God becomes your joy and your peace. And you can learn to see the soul in all beings by learning the art of meditation, and by controlling the senses and passions.

The soul, which is beyond thought, shines equally in the mightiest beast and the tiniest insect. The soul shines equally in people on the farthest island, and in people close at hand. The soul is indifferent to size and race.

Mundaka Upanishad 3:1.1–5, 7

Becoming the sea

Not through listening to lectures, nor through intellectual
debate, nor through studying sacred texts, can the soul be
known. The soul reveals itself to those who yearn to know
the soul. The soul chooses as its own those who choose to
seek the soul.

Not by those lacking courage, not by those lacking determination, not by those lacking self-discipline, can the soul be
known. The soul reveals itself to those who direct their wills
entirely towards the soul.

Those who search for the soul, find the soul. And those
who find the soul, acquire all knowledge; they have no further questions to ask. They see the soul in every living being
whom they encounter; and thus they serve every living being
they encounter. By knowing the soul, they are united with all
beings.

By renouncing worldly knowledge, you acquire spiritual
knowledge. By renouncing worldly life, you attain immortality. By renouncing the pleasures of the body, you are freed
from the pains of the body.

The flowing river is lost in the sea; may you lose yourself
in the soul. The flowing river becomes the sea; may you become the soul.

Mundaka Upanishad 3:2.3–8

Four conditions of the soul

Aum: this is the eternal word. It symbolizes what was, what is, and what shall be. It also represents what is beyond the past, beyond the present, and beyond the future.

God is all; and the soul is God. The soul has four conditions. The first condition is wakefulness, when the senses are turned outwards, focusing on the external world. The second condition is dreaming, when the senses are turned inwards, focusing on past deeds and present desires. The third condition is dreamless sleep, when desires are resting.

The fourth condition is purity. The senses are turned neither outwards nor inwards; there is neither wakefulness nor dreaming. This is the condition of supreme consciousness, when there is complete awareness of the soul. This fourth condition is expressed by the syllable Aum.

Aum is one syllable with three sounds. A stands for the first condition; U for the second condition; M for the third condition. Aum unifies the three conditions in which the soul becomes itself.

Mandukya Upanishad 1–12

THE BHAGAVAD GITA

The *Bhagavad Gita* – the 'Song of the Adorable One' – appears within one of the great Indian epics, the *Mahabharata*, as a dialogue between the hero Arjuna and his charioteer Krishna, on the eve of a great battle. But it was composed separately from the rest of the work; and within it Krishna is the incarnation of God. Indeed, the bulk of it consists of a series of discourses by Krishna on spiritual matters. The main theme is yoga – the attainment of union with the divine. Krishna distinguishes three forms of yoga: the yoga of knowledge; the yoga of action; and the yoga of devotion.

The soul in the body

The soul continues unchanged, as the body passes through childhood, youth and old age; and at death the soul goes to a new body. The wise are not anxious or bewildered by this.

Through the senses the body feels heat and cold, pleasure and pain. They come and they go; and since they are transient, you should endure them with tranquillity. Those who are not perturbed by fleeting sensations, and for whom pleasure and pain are the same, are ready for immortality.

That which is unreal, can never become real; and that which is real, can never become unreal. Those who have seen the boundary between the real and unreal, have acquired all knowledge.

The soul pervades all that exists; yet it cannot be destroyed – no one can kill the soul. From the beginning of time the soul has dwelt in bodies. Though every body is finite in size, the soul is infinite. Though every body dies, the soul is immortal.

If people think that the soul can commit murder, they are mistaken. If people think that the soul within them can be murdered, they are mistaken. The soul cannot kill, nor be killed.

The soul is not born, and does not die.

2.13–20

Fighting in a righteous cause

All living beings must die, and out of death comes new life; since death is inevitable, you should not grieve over it. The soul dwells in all living beings, and the soul cannot die; since death cannot kill the soul, you should not grieve over it.

Do your duty without wavering; there is no greater honour than fighting in a righteous cause. To turn your back on a righteous cause, would be to turn your back on duty and honour; it would be to fall into sin. Your friends would say that you had fled from the fight out of fear; they would forget your great deeds of the past, and treat you with scorn. Your enemies would speak about you with contempt and derision; they would laugh at your reputation for courage. Can any fate be more shameful?

Prepare to fight with peace in your heart. Whether you enjoy pleasure or suffer pain, be at peace. Whether you advance, or are forced back, be at peace. Whether you win or lose, be at peace. If you are at peace within yourself, you cannot sin.

2.27, 30–31, 33–36, 38

The path of yoga

Learn about the path of yoga, which leads from bondage to liberation. It is the eternal path. No step along this path can be reversed; no effort is wasted. Even a small amount of progress brings freedom from fear.

To follow this path requires concentration, in which your only wish is to reach the end. Those who lack concentration, take wrong turnings, and are lost.

Many people speak eloquently about the path of yoga, but have no knowledge of it. They imagine that following the path consists in nothing but learning and expounding sacred texts. Their souls are warped by selfish desires; and they equate the things which they desire, with the end of the path.

To those who understand yoga, sacred texts are as useless as a water tank in the midst of a flood.

Set your heart on the right actions, not on their rewards. Do nothing for the sake of a reward; but never cease to act as you should act. Let your actions be rooted in yoga. Abandon all attachments, and thus be indifferent to success and failure. Yoga brings inner peace.

2.39–43, 46, 47–48

Inner peace

When you abandon every desire that rises up within you, and when you become content with things as they are, then you experience inner peace.

When your mind is untroubled by misfortune, when you desire no pleasures, when your emotions are tranquil, and when you are free from fear and anger, then you experience inner calm.

When you are free from all attachments, when you are indifferent to success and failure, then you experience inner serenity.

When you can withdraw your senses from pleasures of the senses, just as a tortoise withdraws its limbs, then you experience inner wisdom.

When no pleasure and no desire can touch the soul, then you experience the highest state of consciousness.

Yet even those who are close to this state, can suddenly be carried away by a sudden surge of desire. Thus you must learn to meditate, controlling your senses, and focusing yourself entirely on me.

2.55–61

Freedom from aversion and attachment

Those who are focused on the objects of the senses, become attached to those objects. From attachment comes desire; and from desire comes anger; from anger comes confusion of mind; from confusion of mind comes loss of memory; from loss of memory comes loss of intelligence; and from loss of intelligence comes destruction.

But those who can move in the world of the senses, and yet be free from both attachment and aversion, experience inner peace, in which there is no sorrow or sadness. This is wisdom, which arises from knowledge of the soul.

If your mind is distracted by the senses, how can you meditate? If you cannot meditate, how can you experience inner peace? And if you cannot experience inner peace, how can you know joy? When you let your mind follow the senses, they carry away all wisdom – just as storms carry a boat from its course on the sea.

Devote yourself to freeing the senses from attachment and aversion alike. In this way you will dispel the darkness of ignorance – which most people regard as day – and awake to the light of truth.

Rivers flow into the sea, but cannot make the sea overflow. In the same way the streams of impressions from the world of senses will flow into your mind, but they will not make your passions overflow. On the contrary, you will remain calm and tranquil.

2.62–70

The yoga of action

There are two forms of yoga by which perfection may be attained. One form is the yoga of knowledge. The other is the yoga of action.

You cannot attain perfection by merely shirking action. Indeed it is impossible even for a moment to be utterly inactive. All living beings are driven to action by their own natures. Those who withdraw from action, while allowing their minds to dwell on sensual pleasures, are deluding themselves; they can never follow the path to perfection.

Fulfil your duties; action is better than inaction. Indeed, you should strive to maintain the health and strength of your body. Yet selfish action will enslave you. Act selflessly, without any thought of personal gain.

When human beings were created, the obligation of selfless action was also created. God promised that through selfless action human beings would fulfil their deepest desires.

Good people, who share the fruits of their work, are freed from all their sins. But those who keep the fruits of their work for themselves, consume sin. Every selfless action is inspired by God; he is present in every good deed. All life turns on this truth.

3.1–10, 13–16

Setting an example

The actions of outstanding people set an example which others try to follow; their behaviour is the standard by which others judge themselves.

I gain nothing from my own actions. I act continuously for the well-being of others; but I am not motivated by any need of my own. If I ever refrained from working, everyone would immediately stop working also – and the world would be thrown into chaos, which would lead to its destruction.

Ignorant people work only for their own profit; wise people work for the welfare of others, without thought for themselves. By your own actions demonstrate to the ignorant the joy of work. Act always in accordance with the soul; perform all your actions out of devotion to me.

Those who act in accordance with the soul, are released from the consequences of sin. But those who violate the soul by their action, cause themselves terrible suffering.

In deciding how they should act, wise people recognize the limitations of their own natures. They also recognize that at any time feelings of hate or lust may rise up within them. They are constantly watching for these obstacles in their path; and thus they never stumble on them.

Do the work that your nature allows you to do; and never try to do work that suits other people better.

3.21–26, 31–35

Slaying selfish desires

Selfish desires and anger bind us to selfish deeds. They are the enemies of the soul.

A fire may be covered by smoke; a mirror may be obscured by dust; the embryo lies deep within the womb. In the same way wisdom is hidden by selfish desire – hidden by the urge to satisfy appetites that can never be satisfied.

Selfish desires are found in the senses, the emotions, and the intellect; they bury the mind in delusion. Fight them with all your strength. Control your senses, your emotions and your intellect; vanquish your enemies; conquer all that strives to conquer wisdom.

The power of the senses is formidable. But the emotions are more powerful than the senses; and the intellect is more powerful than the emotions. The soul is the master of the intellect. So let the soul rule the intellect – and then you will slay all selfish desires.

3.37–43

Manifest in bodily form

You and I have both passed through many births. You have forgotten your past lives, whereas I remember mine. I am unborn and eternal; I am the lord of all living beings. Yet through my own power I make myself manifest in bodily form. When righteousness is weak in the world, and the purpose of life has been forgotten, I appear. I am born in every age, to uphold that which is good, to destroy that which is evil, and to teach people how they should act.

Those who know me, and identify me with the soul, break free from the cycle of birth and death. When they die, they are not reborn, but are brought into unity with me. By surrendering to me, people are saved from attachment, fear and desire; they are purified by the fire of my presence.

As people come to me. I welcome them. All paths lead to me. I decreed the law of cause and effect; I decided that sinful actions should cause suffering, and righteous actions should cause joy. But I am beyond cause and effect; I am not bound by the consequences of actions, because I am attached to nothing. Those who understand this, and emulate it, are set free; they engage in righteous action for its own sake, without any selfish concern for its results.

4.5–11, 13–15

Worship through action

What is action, and what is inaction? This question has confused even the greatest thinkers. The wise see that there is action in the midst of inaction, and inaction in the midst of action. Thus they find peace in every act which they perform.

If you are wise, you undertake every action without any anxiety about its result; your selfish desires have been consumed in the fire of truth. You expect nothing from your actions, and you rely on nothing; you have no hopes, so you cannot be disappointed. You surrender all prospect of personal gain, and you act only for the sake of the action itself. You are thus master of yourself, and you are in no danger of committing sin.

In this way you rise above the conflicts of earthly life. You compete with no one in your actions; you are indifferent to success and failure; and you are equally content with any outcome. You act only in the spirit of service.

Thus your actions are an offering to God; and through your actions you draw closer to God. You worship God in all you do.

Some people offer material sacrifices to God; but God prefers the sacrifice of selfless action. Some people deny themselves all pleasures of the senses; but God prefers the senses to be used in the service of others.

4.16–26

The leaves of the lotus

Those who practice the yoga of knowledge, transcend all duality. They like nothing, and they dislike nothing; they desire nothing, and they fear nothing. They are free from the bondage of self-will. Ignorant people think that the yoga of knowledge and the yoga of action are utterly different, and even opposed; but wise people recognize that both lead to the same goal. The person who is adept in the yoga of knowledge, will attain the rewards of selfless action; the person who is adept in the yoga of action, will attain the rewards of divine knowledge.

The yoga of knowledge is difficult to practice without any action. So those who wish to make rapid progress on the path to God, dedicate themselves to the service of others. They learn to master the senses and to conquer selfish desires; and in this way they perceive the soul in all living beings.

As people practice the yoga of action, a moment comes when they think: 'I am not performing these actions.' In seeing and hearing, smelling and touching, eating and walking, sleeping and breathing, even opening and closing the eyes, they realize that the body has become the servant of the soul.

The leaves of the lotus remain clean and dry even in the muddiest water. In the same way those who practice the yoga of action, offering all their actions to God, cannot be touched by sin. In every situation they remain pure.

5.3–11

Treating all equally

God is not the author of either the good deeds or the evil deeds which a person performs. People do evil deeds when their inherent wisdom is clouded by ignorance. But this cloud is dispelled by knowledge of the soul, which dwells within every living being. This knowledge shines like the sun, revealing God himself. When you acquire it, you are no longer capable of committing sin; you have attained the supreme goal of human existence, which is unity with God.

The soul is present in equal measure in the priest and the outcast, in the elephant, the cow and the dog. Thus knowledge of the soul prompts you to treat all living beings with equal respect. You feel at ease in the company of every kind of person.

With your mind rooted in God, you see his perfection everywhere. You are neither elated by good fortune, nor depressed by bad fortune. Your intellect is clear and calm, and is free from all delusion. You depend on no one and nothing, but you are at one with everyone and everything. And thus you experience profound inner peace, which nothing can shatter.

5.15–21

The essence of yoga

The pleasures of the senses have a beginning and an end; for this reason they lead to misery. Do not look for happiness in them. When desire for pleasure rises up within your body, suppress it. When anger surges within the body, calm it. In this way you will attain peace and joy; you will discover the light of God shining within you.

Sin and conflict are diseases, which destroy those who are afflicted with them. Heal yourself of sin and conflict by working for the well-being of others. This is what wise people have always taught. Free yourself from anger and desire, which are the causes of sin and conflict, and thereby make yourself whole. This is the essence of yoga; this is the means by which you come to know the soul, and thereby attain the highest spiritual state.

Learn to meditate. Close your eyes; calm your breathing; and focus your attention on the centre of consciousness. Thus you will master the senses, the emotions and the intellect – and thereby free yourself from desire and anger.

Meditate upon me. I am the friend of all living beings. I am the ruler of the universe. I am the object of all true worship. I am the goal to which yoga is directed. Through me, and me alone, you can find peace and joy.

5.22–29

The summit of consciousness

Those who do not work for an earthly reward, but who do the work that needs to be done, are the true yogis. But those who spend their time lighting sacred fires and offering sacrifices, are not true yogis. Genuine renunciation and selfless service are one and the same; selfless service consists in renouncing all attachment to the results of work.

If you wish to climb the mountain of spiritual knowledge, you must follow the path of selfless work; and when you reach the summit, you will find yourself in the land of perfect peace. Free yourself from all attachment to the results of your work, and from desires for external objects.

By the power of your own will, lift yourself up; never let yourself be brought down by self-will. The will can be the true friend of the soul; the will can also be its true enemy. To those who are striving to conquer desire and attachment, the will is the soul's friend; to those who are indifferent to the soul, the will is the soul's enemy.

God is revealed in the consciousness of those who have mastered themselves. In cold and heat, in pleasure and pain, in honour and disgrace, they enjoy the peace of God. To them a clod of dirt and a lump of gold are the same. They have reached the summit of consciousness.

6. 1–9

Learning to meditate

Day by day you should seek the soul through meditation. Learn to master your body and your mind. Teach yourself to hope for nothing and to desire nothing.

For your daily meditation find a place of solitude, where no one can find you. It should be clean, and it should be neither too high nor too low. Lay a piece of cloth or deer-skin on the ground, and sit down. Once you are seated comfortably, strive to calm your thoughts. Focus your mind on a single point. Do not allow any impure thoughts to disturb your mind. Hold your body, neck and head upright in a straight line, and keep your eyes from wandering.

Now let all your fears dissolve into the soul, and dedicate all your desires to God. Fix the mind on me; think of me as your only goal; find joy and peace in the image of me. Unify yourself with the soul that dwells within you.

Those who eat too much or too little, and those who sleep too much or too little, will not succeed in meditation. Equally those who work too hard, or who rest too long, will not succeed. So be temperate in eating and sleeping, in work and recreation.

Through meditation every sorrow ceases, and every selfish desire fades away.

6. 10–18

The steady flame

When you have calmed the mind through meditation, the soul will reveal itself. You will behold the soul by means of the soul; and it will appear as bright and as steady as the flame of a lamp in a cave. And as the soul reveals itself, you will experience the joy and peace of complete fulfilment. This joy transcends the senses, and so can never be taken away. You will desire nothing, so no desire can be frustrated; and even the gravest misfortune will not shake you. You will abide in eternal truth.

This is the way of yoga. Follow it with determination and with enthusiasm. When you renounce worldly desires, do so with all your heart. When you exert your will over your senses, do so with all your strength. Little by little, with patience and with effort, you will win.

From time to time your mind will wander, restlessly seeking pleasures in the external world. Whenever this happens, grasp your mind firmly, and turn it inwards, directing it towards the soul. Train the mind to relax within the soul. Teach the mind to enjoy the peace which comes through resting in the soul.

As you come to know the soul within yourself, so you will perceive that the soul pervades the entire world. Through meditation your consciousness will become unified with the consciousness of every living being. You will become aware of my presence in every man and woman, animal and bird. All that lives, abides in me.

6.19–27, 29–30

Knowledge and action

The mind is restless, impetuous, and turbulent; yet it can be controlled. By frequent and regular meditation, and by striving to detach yourself from all external objects, you can conquer the mind. Those who lack self-discipline, and therefore fail to meditate as they should, will not make progress. But those who practise meditation day by day, and who keep constant watch over themselves, will eventually attain the supreme goal.

Yet even those who fail to control their minds, will be saved – so long as they serve others. No one who does good works, will ever come to a bad end. When good people die, they go to that realm where righteousness is rewarded. Then they are born again in good homes. Their new parents may themselves do good works; or they may be people who practise meditation – although this is rare. In either case the wisdom acquired in previous lives will be re-awakened, and they will strive even harder to know the soul. Indeed, the strength which they gained through past spiritual exertions, will drive them forward. Thus through constant effort over many lifetimes, they too will attain the supreme goal.

The yoga of knowledge is superior to any kind of self-mortification; and it is also superior to selfless service. Therefore I urge you to meditate, putting your whole trust in me.

6.35–36, 40–47

A necklace of jewels

When you meditate, focus your mind entirely on me. Depend on me completely. I shall dispel all your doubts; and I shall reveal myself fully to you, so that you and I are as one.

I shall give you both wisdom and vision. When you possess these, you will possess all knowledge; you will realize that there is nothing else for you to know.

Only one person in many thousands sincerely strives for perfection; yet even amongst those striving for perfection, very few attain it – very few come to know me fully.

There are eight visible forms of my nature: earth, water, fire, air, space, emotions, intellect, and the sense of self. But beyond my visible nature, I have a higher, invisible spirit. This spirit sustains the entire universe, and is the source of all life.

These two parts of my nature are the womb of creation. I brought the universe to birth; and in me the universe will come to an end. There is nothing in existence separate from me. The entire universe is suspended from me, like a necklace of jewels.

7.1–7

Penetrating the veil of mystery

I am the taste of pure water, and the radiance of the sun and the moon. I am Aum, the sacred syllable, which is heard in silence. I am the courage that inspires heroes. I am the fragrance of the plants that grow in the earth; and I am the heat of fire. I am the life of all that lives; and I am the striving of all who wish to know me.

I am the seed of eternal life. I am the intelligence of the intelligent. I am the beauty of that which is beautiful. I am the glory of those who are noble. I am the strength of the strong. I am the pure desire for righteousness.

The three states of consciousness have been ordained by me: the state of peaceful brightness; the state of restless twilight; and the state of lifeless darkness. I am not in these states, but they come from me. These three states deceive the world: people fail to look beyond them to me, and so fail to see that I alone am supreme and immortal. The three states are the veil of mystery which I have made, and which is hard to penetrate. Some succeed in going through this veil, and hence find me. But most are deluded by it, and so continue to perform evil deeds.

7.8–15

True worship

There are four kinds of people who are good, and who love
me: those burdened by sorrow; those seeking knowledge;
those striving to achieve life's purpose; and those with vision.
The greatest of these are those with vision; they are unwavering in their devotion to me, and they are always at one
with me. I love men and women with vision, and they love
me. All those following the way of yoga are blessed; but
those with vision are especially blessed, because they perceive
the soul everywhere and within everyone.

There are people whose vision has been distorted by numerous desires. They pursue these desires; and their religion
is merely performing various rituals.

People put their faith in many things; and people always
live according to their faith. So those who put their faith in
that which is false or corrupt, will lead false or corrupt lives.
Many people have a false image of me, identifying me with
various bodily forms, and not recognizing my higher nature.
They cannot see through the veil of mystery which surrounds
me; and so they cannot see that I am unborn and changeless.
I know everything about the past, the present, and the future;
but no one knows me completely.

But those who always strive to do good, and who are free
from every inclination to do wrong, truly worship me.

7.16–26, 28

God's spirit and power

God is supreme and eternal. The soul is God's spirit which
dwells in every living being. God's power brings all living
beings into existence, and sustains them. The bodies of all
living beings are made of matter, which in time passes away;
but the soul is eternal.

8.3–4

The moment of death

Those who think of me at the moment of death, will come to me. Do not doubt this. Whatever occupies a person's mind at the moment of death, indicates the destination of that person after death. This is because people's dying thoughts reveal the true spiritual state.

Therefore think of me at all times. When you are in the midst of battle, keep me in your mind. Let your intellect and your emotions dwell on me. In order to achieve this single-ness of mind, you must meditate regularly.

I am the poet, and the universe is my poem. I am the supreme ruler. I am smaller than the smallest atom; yet I support the entire universe with my arms. I shine as brightly as the sun; yet I am beyond darkness. Devote yourself entirely to me, and meditate upon me constantly; concentrate your attention at the point between your eyebrows which is the centre of consciousness. Then you will know me as the supreme Lord; and at the moment of death your mind will be fixed on me.

At the moment of death the gates of your senses will close, and your mind will withdraw into the heart. As you think of me, direct all your energy upwards to the head. Repeat the divine syllable Aum, which symbolizes God. Then you will leave the body, and attain the supreme goal.

8.5–10, 12–13

Unity with God

Those who through the practice of yoga constantly think about me, can easily attain me. Such people make their lives perfect; in their perfection they discover me; through discovering me they are unified with me; and through unity with me they are freed from suffering and death. All living beings on earth are subject to death and rebirth, except those in union with me.

Those in union with me know that my day lasts a thousand aeons, and my night lasts a thousand aeons. They know that all visible things arise from that which is invisible, and will disappear into that which is invisible. They know that the countless living beings on earth have been created by me, and will be destroyed by me; and that the process of creation and destruction will be repeated again and again. They know that beyond mortality there is immortality; that when all living things have been destroyed, life remains. And they know that those who attain immortality, can never return to mortality.

Those in union with me know that the soul pervades all that exists; and that the soul can be found through undivided love.

8. 14–22

The paths of light and darkness

There are two paths which may be followed at the moment of death; one leads to rebirth, and the other to liberation.

There are six months of the year when the sun is growing brighter and the days are growing longer. These represent the path to liberation. There are six months when the sun is growing dimmer, and the days are growing shorter. These represent the path to rebirth.

There are two weeks in the month when the moon is growing larger and its light is increasing. These represent the path to liberation. There are two weeks when the moon is growing smaller and its light is decreasing. These represent the path to rebirth.

These two paths, the path of light and the path of darkness, have always existed. And at the moment of death some have followed the path of light towards liberation, while others have followed the path of darkness towards rebirth.

Once you know these two paths, you can never again be deluded. And you can attain this knowledge through the practice of meditation. There is merit in studying sacred texts; there is merit in selfless service; there is merit in self-mortification; and there is merit in giving to the needy. But the practice of meditation carries you beyond all these, to the place where God himself resides.

8.23–28

As the winds

I pervade the entire universe. I am invisible; yet I am present in all that is visible. All living beings exist through me; yet my existence does not depend on them. I dwell in all living beings; but they do not dwell in me. I am the source of all life, and I sustain all life; yet I do not need support or sustenance. As the winds blow through the vastness of space, so I am the breath of all that breathes.

At the end of the present aeon all beings will return to me; and at the beginning of the next aeon I shall bring them back to birth. I have called back all beings at the end of every aeon; and I have brought them to birth at the beginning of every aeon. I am not attached to these actions, or to any actions; nothing binds me, so nothing can disturb me.

I ordained the laws of nature; and I watch over them with my vigilant eye. I set the world in motion; and I ensure that it remains on the course I set.

Ignorant people only look at the appearance of things, so they do not see me as I truly am. Thus they do not realize that I am the ruler of all beings. Ignorant people may study all kinds of subjects; but their knowledge is mere delusion, and their thoughts are empty. Wise people discern me, because they have trained their minds to meditate on me. And they worship me as I am, never wavering in their devotion to me; they sing my glory.

9.4−14

The divine being

Those who practise the yoga of knowledge – who seek spiritual wisdom – worship me both as one and as many, because they perceive that I am present in all things. They see my face everywhere, so they worship me in everything.

I am the ritual and the sacrifice. I am the medicine that heals the body, and the chant that calms the mind. I am the offering, the fire which consumes it, and the one to whom it is offered.

I am the father and the mother of the universe, and the grandparents too. I am the Creator of all that exists. I am the sum of all knowledge. I am the one who purifies that which is corrupt. I am the syllable Aum. I am every sacred text.

I am the goal of life, and the one who guides living beings towards that goal. I am the silent witness, observing all that happens. I am the friend of all living beings; I am their shelter; I am the place of peace to which they can retreat. I am the beginning, the middle, and the end of all that occurs. I am the seed of eternity.

I am the heat of the sun, and the wetness of the rain. I am the life of living and the death of dying. I am immortality. I am what is, and I am what is not.

9.15–19

The unity of religions

There are people who perform all the ancient rituals, who offer all the sacrifices which the sacred texts prescribe, who drink the sacred drinks, who keep themselves from committing any sin, and who pray regularly. They will be rewarded for their efforts: they will go to a realm above the earth, and enjoy many blessings and pleasures. But when these blessings and pleasures are complete, they will return to earth, and be trapped once more in the cycle of death and rebirth. Performing rituals cannot liberate a person from the chains of desire.

But those who worship me, who meditate upon me constantly, and who live in perfect harmony with me, will attain perfection. I shall not merely provide for their needs, but I shall give them far more.

I make no distinction between one religion and another. People may worship me in any form they wish. The form of worship does not matter to me; my only concern is the quality of love which is expressed in worship. I accept every kind of worship, because I am supreme.

9.20—24

The equality of all people

People may offer me merely a leaf, or a flower, or even a little water; I shall accept it, so long as it is offered in a spirit of devotion. Offerings are merely symbols, which in themselves do not concern me; I want a pure heart and a mind hungry for truth. Whatever you do, or eat, or give, let it be an offering to me; and whatever you suffer, then suffer it for my sake.

In this way you will break free from the bonds of cause and effect. You will be free from all interest in the consequences of action, because you will be free from desire and fear. You will be free to come to me.

I look upon all living beings equally; I do not love one being more and another being less. But those who love me, live in me, and I come to life in them. Even the worst sinners become holy when they turn to me, and worship me with all their hearts and minds. Soon their wickedness is turned into righteousness, their corruption is made pure, and they become tranquil and serene.

All those who devote themselves to me, will attain the supreme goal – regardless of race, sex, or class. Those whom society scorns, are equal in my sight to those whom society exalts. You have been born into a world where suffering is constant and pleasures are fleeting. Give all your love to me; fill your mind with me; serve me with all your strength; seek me with all your heart. Then you and I will be united in joy.

9.26–34

The lamp of truth

The angels do not know my origin, because I am the origin of the angels themselves. Even the wisest sages do not know my origin, because all their wisdom comes from me. Those who recognize me as the ruler of all that is, and who understand that I have no birth or beginning, know the truth – and are thus free from all evil.

I am the source of intelligence, wisdom, understanding, forgiveness, truth, self-control, and serenity. I am the source of pleasure and pain, birth and death, fear and courage, honour and disgrace. I am the source of gentleness, generosity, patience, contentment, and endurance. Every virtue found in any living being comes from me.

The original sages were taught by me. The first human beings were born from my mind, and given life by my power; and from these first humans all men and women in the entire world are descended. Those who acknowledge my glory and power are at one with me.

From me every species of living being has evolved. The wise reflect on this, and worship me with devotion. Their thoughts flow towards me, and their vitality flows from me. They teach one another, talking constantly about me. They are joyful and happy.

I give spiritual wisdom to all who love me. I dispel the darkness of ignorance, and light within them the lamp of truth.

10.2–11

The lion, the eagle and the crocodile

I am the soul in the heart of all that exists. I am the birth of all beings, the life of all beings, and the death of all beings.

In the sky during the day I am the sun. During a storm I am the wind. In the sky at night I am the moon.

Among the senses I am the mind. In all living beings I am the consciousness.

Among the material things of the world I am the wealth. Among the elements I am the fire, which purifies every object. In the mountain ranges I am the summits.

Among priests I am the chief priest. Among stretches of water I am the ocean. Among sages I am the teacher. Among words I am Aum, the eternal word.

Among trees I am the tree of life. Among men I am the king. Among weapons I am the thunderbolt. Among virtues I am love.

On land I am the lion. In the air I am the eagle. In the river I am the crocodile.

10.20–28, 30

The science of sciences

Of all the sciences, I am the science of the soul. When people engage in debate, I am the logic of their arguments. When people speak or write, I am the grammar that holds their words together.

I am time, which never ends. I am the Creator, who sees all. I am the destroyer, who brings death. I am the future, deciding what will happen.

I am that which makes a woman beautiful. I am the qualities in her appearance which attract attention. I am the sweetness of her speech. I am her capacity to ponder on events. I am her loyalty to her family. And I am her patience with the failings of others.

In music I am the melody, and in poetry I am the metre. Among months, I am the first of the year. Among seasons I am spring, when flowers burst forth.

I am the chance in a gambler's dice. I am the brightness of a lamp. I am the effort of those who strive. I am the victory of those who win. I am the goodness of those who are righteous.

I am the sceptre of those who rule. I am the shrewdness of those who lead. I am the silence of those whose voice is never heard. And I am the wisdom of the wise.

There is no end to what I am. Wherever you find strength, or beauty, or knowledge, or power, you find me.

10.32–36, 38, 40–41

God's universal form

Look at the thousands of different forms which I take. Look at the innumerable shapes and colours of these forms. Look at my finest forms, such as the sun in the sky, and the flashes of lightning during storms. Every object in the entire universe is my body; and every movement in the universe is a movement of my body. Yet with your physical eyes you can never see me in myself; so I must give you spiritual eyes with which to look upon me.

With the eyes that I give you, you can see my universal form, which has no beginning and no end. My universal form cannot be seen without eyes bestowed by me. It cannot be seen through knowledge of sacred texts, nor through sacrifices, nor through acts of charity, nor through rituals, nor even through the most rigorous asceticism.

Do not be anxious. Do not be frightened of my universal form. Your heart will be satisfied, and all fear dispelled.

Love me with unfailing devotion. Then you will know me and see me. Those who make vision of me their only goal, and dedicate their whole lives to that goal, will attain union with me.

11.5–8, 47–49, 54–55

Devotion, knowledge and service

Some people love me with all their hearts, and worship me with unwavering faith. They practise the yoga of devotion.

Others seek me as the sublime reality, the transcendental truth which has no name or form. They contemplate me as that which cannot be seen, and which is beyond the reach of thought and feeling. They subdue their senses, still their minds, and fill their hearts with goodwill towards all living beings. They practise the yoga of knowledge.

The path trodden by those practising the yoga of knowledge is hard and hazardous. Yet those who travel along it with unflagging effort, swiftly reach me. And when they reach me, I release them from the cycle of birth and death. Their consciousness becomes my consciousness.

Focus your mind upon me, and you will know me. If you cannot do this at once, then learn to do it through regular meditation. If you lack the self-discipline for meditation, then engage yourself in my work, which is the selfless service of others. If you are unable to do even this, then devote your heart to me, surrendering to me the fruits of all your actions. By one of these three means you will attain inner peace.

12.2−11

Loved by God

I shall describe the people whom I love. They have goodwill towards all living beings, and are incapable of ill will. They are friendly and compassionate. They regard nothing as their own possession, and want no position of power for themselves. They are indifferent to both pleasure and pain. They are patient, contented, and self-controlled. They are firm in faith, and their hearts and minds are utterly devoted to me.

Their serenity is constant, and cannot be disturbed by others; on the contrary, their presence makes others feel serene. They are not elated by good fortune, nor depressed by misfortune. They do not compete with others, and they have no fear of failure.

They are not attracted to particular people and places, nor are they repelled by particular people and places. They are both selfless and efficient in all their actions. They have no desire for pleasure, and no fear of pain. They never grieve over the death of others or the loss of material goods; they accept with equanimity every event as it occurs.

They love friends and enemies equally. They are not encouraged by praise nor discouraged by blame. Whether they are honoured or despised, they remain perfectly calm. Within their hearts there is silence.

These are the people whom I especially love.

12.13–19

The field and its knower

A body is called a field. Those who understand their bodies, are called knowers of the field. You should know that I am the knower of all the fields in the world. And when particular people know their fields, I am that which knows. To know the field is true wisdom.

I shall explain briefly the nature of the field, and how changes take place within it. I shall also describe the knower of the field, and the power which the knower possesses. These truths have been expounded by sages in many different ways.

The field is made up of the senses and the organs of the senses; the five elements; the sense of self; the intellect and the imagination; and energy which enables each part to function. Change can take place in the field through desire and revulsion, pleasure and pain, intelligence and will.

Those who know the field, are free from pride and deceit. They are gentle and forgiving, righteous and pure, strong and self-controlled. They are detached from the objects of the senses. They are not disturbed by disease and old age; and the prospect of death does not frighten them. They love their families, but do not feel possessive towards them. They enjoy solitude, and are not swayed by the opinions of the crowd.

13. 1—10

The light of the soul

I shall tell you of the soul. The soul is God – who is immortal and infinite, who has no beginning and will have no end, and who both exists and does not exist. Those who know the soul, are immortal.

The soul dwells in every living being, and in every part of every living being; it dwells in the hand and the foot, the skull and the mouth, the eye and the ear. Although it does not itself have senses, it shines through every sense. It is completely independent, yet all beings depend on it.

The soul is both near every living being, and far from every being. The soul is both inside and outside every living being. The soul is the cause of movement, but does not itself move. The soul is one, yet has innumerable forms. The soul creates, preserves, and destroys.

The soul is the light of every light; and its light transcends the duality of brightness and darkness. The soul is the light of knowledge; and its light is also the goal of knowledge. In the soul the subject and object of knowledge are one.

13.12–17

Three forms of yoga

There are three forms of yoga, by which immortality is attained. The first is the yoga of knowledge, which requires regular meditation. The second is the yoga of devotion. And the third is the yoga of selfless service.

Many people do not know these forms of yoga by name; but under the guidance of an enlightened teacher they practice one of them – and they too pass beyond death.

13.24–25

Seeing truly

If you see the soul in every living being, you see truly. If you
see immortality in the heart of every mortal being, you see
truly. If you see God within every man and woman, then you
can never do harm to any man or woman. If you see God in
yourself, then you attain perfection.

When you see the soul in every living being, you see that
all actions are performed by the soul's energy – though the
soul itself does not act. You see that the soul inspires every
movement – though the soul itself does not move. When you
see that amidst the variety of living beings the soul is the
unity, then you attain fulfilment.

The soul has no birth; it cannot be divided into parts; and
it has no death. It dwells in the body, but it is not touched
by the body. It pervades the universe, but is not affected by
anything in the universe. The soul can never be corrupted or
stained.

As the sun lights up the world, the soul lights up the
body. Those who possess the eye of wisdom, can distinguish
the soul from the body – and therefore they can break free
from the body.

13.27–34

Peace, assertion and passivity

I shall tell you about the knowledge that transcends all earthly knowledge. It is through this knowledge that the holy people attain perfection. Those who rely totally on this knowledge, become part of me; after death they will never again be re-born, nor will they be destroyed.

I am the womb of the universe; and in me is the seed of all that exists. From me all beings come to birth. Thus I am the mother and father of every living being.

Peace, assertion and passivity are the three forces which bind the soul to the body. Peace, which is pure and free from sorrow, produces health and happiness – and binds the soul to these things. Assertion produces passion and action – and binds the soul to these things. And passivity produces ignorance and delusion – and binds the soul to these things.

At times peace prevails over assertion and passivity; at times assertion prevails over peace and passivity; and at times passivity prevails over peace and assertion. When peace prevails, wisdom shines through the body; when assertion prevails, the person dashes about pursuing selfish desires; when passivity prevails, the person is lazy, confused, and easily infatuated.

14.1–13

Wisdom, desire and confusion

If peace prevails at the moment of death, the person will be reborn possessing great wisdom. If assertion prevails at the moment of death, the person will be reborn as an artisan or labourer. If passivity prevails at the moment of death, the person will be reborn as a useless layabout.

The fruit of deeds prompted by peace is happiness. The fruit of deeds prompted by assertion is suffering. The fruit of deeds prompted by passivity is ignorance.

From peace comes wisdom. From assertion comes desire. From passivity comes confusion.

Those in whom peace prevails, move steadily upwards. Those in whom assertion prevails, remain as they are. Those in whom passivity prevails, move steadily downwards.

The wise recognize that all action is prompted by peace, assertion or passivity – or a mixture of them. This recognition enables them to rise above these forces, and to enter union with God. These forces bind the soul to the body; so by rising above them, they leave behind the cycle of birth, decay and death, and attain immortality.

14.14–20

Rising above bodily forces

Those who have risen above the forces of peace, assertion and passivity, are unmoved by them. They are unmoved by the happiness which peace produces; they are unmoved by the suffering which assertion produces; and they are unmoved by the confusion which passivity produces. They are neither attracted by the forces of peace, assertion and passivity, nor repelled by them.

Thus you should learn to recognize these forces within yourself. You should observe how they bind the soul to the body. In this way you can learn to master them; and once you have mastered them, you will no longer be disturbed by them.

You will no longer desire pleasure, nor will you fear pain. You will no longer desire praise, nor will you fear disgrace. You will no longer desire others to be kind to you, nor will you fear the unkindness of others. A lump of clay and a piece of gold will be the same to you. You will treat friends and enemies alike. You will give up every kind of selfish activity.

You will know God, love God, and serve God; you will be in union with God. I am the embodiment of God; I am the eternal fountain of life – and I never run dry. The law of righteousness is my law; and my joy lasts for ever.

14.22–26

The tree of death and rebirth

There is a tree of transmigration – a tree of death and rebirth. Its roots are above the sky, and its branches are here on earth. Its leaves are sacred texts; and those who understand these texts, understand the essence of the tree. Its buds are the pleasures of the senses.

The true dimensions of this tree cannot be seen from the earth; human beings cannot see where its roots begin and its branches end. But you can cut it down with the sharp axe of detachment. And once you have done this, you can find the path that leads to the eternal spring, from which the entire universe flowed long ago.

As you wield the sharp axe of detachment, you will destroy pride, and free yourself from selfish desire; you will slice through the duality of pleasure and pain. And as the tree falls, God's light will become visible; neither the sun, nor the moon, nor fire can add to that light.

15.1–6

The author of sacred texts

I have entered this world in bodily form. I have acquired senses, the power of action, and a mind. Just as the wind carries scent from place to place, so I take my body from place to place. I use my ears to hear, my eyes to see, my nose to smell, my tongue to taste, and my skin to touch; and, although I am divine, I allow myself to enjoy the pleasures of the senses.

I am the soul which dwells in the heart of every person and every living being. Those who practise yoga, find me within their own hearts; but those who do not practise yoga, will never find me, even if they search for me.

Those who know me in their hearts, also see me in the brightness of the sun, which lights up the world; they see me in the gleam of the moon, and in the flames of fire. They see me in the power which enables living beings to move. They see me in the water that nourishes the plants growing in the earth. When they observe a person or an animal breathing, they see me in the breath. They feel me in the heat of the stomach which digests food.

They recognize me as the power of memory and understanding. And they acknowledge me as the author of every sacred text.

14.7–15

The deepest mystery

In this world there are two orders of being, the perishable and the imperishable. The perishable is all that is visible. The imperishable is the invisible substance of all that is visible.

But above and beyond the perishable and the imperishable is the supreme soul. The supreme soul created the universe; and having created the universe, the supreme soul entered it, and sustains it.

I am the supreme soul. Every sacred text praises me, and recognizes me as transcending the perishable and the imperishable. Those who encounter me, and see me as the supreme soul, have eyes of truth. Those who worship and adore me with unwavering devotion, have hearts of truth.

I am revealing to you the deepest mystery. When you have fully understood my words, your task in this world is complete.

14.16–19

The divine tendency

Be brave, casting aside all fear. Be pure in heart. Never waver in your determination to understand the truth. Give freely to those in need. Speak with honesty, and act with sincerity. Take delight in serving others. Study the sacred texts. Find joy in detaching yourself from pleasures of the senses. Do not become angry at the failings of others, and never harm any living being. Be compassionate and gentle, and take every opportunity to do good. When you have been wronged, forgive the wrongdoer quickly. Avoid any kind of malice or pride. If you follow this advice, then you will fulfil your divine destiny; you will be living in accordance with the divine tendency within you.

But there is also a demonic tendency within you; and if you allow this tendency to influence you, then you will destroy yourself. The demonic tendency inclines you towards hypocrisy and rudeness, conceit and anger, cruelty and ignorance.

The divine qualities lead to freedom; the demonic qualities lead to bondage. Do not be anxious; the divine tendency is stronger within you than the demonic tendency.

16. 1—5

The demonic tendency

Those who surrender to the demonic tendency, lose all sense of right and wrong; they cannot distinguish between purity and corruption, nor between truth and falsehood.

They declare: 'There is no God, no truth, no spiritual dimension and no moral law. Living beings are conceived out of lust; and gratifying our lusts is all that matters. How can any intelligent person disagree?' Holding such a distorted view, and possessing so little insight, they are enemies of all that lives.

They are hypocritical and proud, arrogant and conceited. They are deluded, and they cling fiercely to their delusions. Their desires are insatiable; and when they cannot satisfy all their desires, they satisfy the most corrupt and unclean. They are frightened of death; yet nothing can shake their conviction that life is no more than lust.

They are constantly devising schemes to outwit their rivals; and they are constantly anxious about the schemes their rivals may be devising. Driven by anger and greed, they will sink to any depth in order to gain greater wealth.

Every day they look at their wealth, and say: 'This is mine; and today I shall add to it. In becoming rich I have impoverished others; today I shall make more people poor. Am I not like God? I have everything I want, and can do anything I want.'

16.7–15

Downwards and upwards

Those who surrender to their demonic tendencies – who are selfish and arrogant, angry and envious – abuse my presence within them. And they also abuse my presence in those they encounter.

When they die, I put them in the wombs of mothers who have also surrendered to their demonic tendencies. Thus they suffer miserable childhoods. And if they continue to surrender to their demonic tendencies, they are reborn once again with parents who are cruel and malicious. Thus life by life they move downwards.

There are three gates to this hell: lust, anger and greed. Renounce all three. If you never approach any of these gates, then life by life you will move upwards, until you attain the supreme goal.

There is a fourth gate: treating sacred texts with contempt. This too destroys all prospect of happiness and joy. Let the sacred texts be your guide in what you do and what you refrain from doing. Study their teachings carefully; and then act in accordance with them.

16.18–24

Inherent faith

All people are born with faith. This inherent faith arises from one of the three forces which bind the body to the soul: peace, assertion, and passivity. And the nature of faith depends on the force from which it arises.

Those whose faith arises from peace, worship God in his various forms. Those whose faith arises from assertion, worship power and wealth. And those whose faith arises from passivity, worship ghostly spirits.

Some people invent harsh austerities for themselves. Their lusts and desires are twisted, so they take pleasure in torturing their bodies. Their real desire is to torture the soul within the body. Their minds are shrouded in darkness.

The three kinds of faith express themselves in the food people eat and the sacrifices they offer. Those whose faith arises from peace, enjoy food that is mild and nourishing. Those whose faith arises from assertion, enjoy food that is salty or bitter, sour or spicy. Those whose faith arises from passivity, enjoy food that is overcooked and stale.

Those whose faith arises from peace, offer sacrifices out of devotion to God, without thought of reward. Those whose faith arises from assertion, perform sacrifices to impress other people. Those whose faith arises from passivity, offer sacrifices merely out of habit, in a slovenly manner.

17.2−13

Self-discipline

Those whose faith arises from peace, discipline their bodies: they are pure and righteous in their behaviour; they control their sexual urges; and they are never violent. They discipline their speech: they speak with honesty; they are invariably courteous, never using harsh words; and they are always willing to share their knowledge. And they discipline their minds: they are calm and gentle, tranquil and compassionate.

Those whose faith arises from assertion, use their bodies, their speech and their minds in order to gain respect, honour and admiration. Those whose faith arises from passivity, use their bodies, speech and mind to gain power over others, or, through harsh austerities, to gain power over themselves.

Those whose faith arises from peace, give generously to others because it is right to be generous; they have no thought of return; and they give in a manner that best suits the recipient. Those whose faith arises from assertion, are reluctant to give; and they only do so when they expect some favour in return. Those whose faith arises from passivity, are insensitive to the needs of others; and when they give, they do so without affection or respect.

17.14–22

Aum, Tat and Sat

Aum, Tat, Sat. Each of these syllables represent God – from whom came the sacred texts.

Those who love God, begin every activity with the syllable Aum. When they start to perform a sacrifice, when they are about to help someone, and when they are preparing to meditate, they say this syllable.

Those who have no thought of reward for what they do, add the syllable Tat. For them the purpose of performing sacrifices, of serving others, and of meditating, is to attain liberation from the cycle of birth and death.

Those who understand all goodness and truth, add the syllable Sat. And they utter this syllable at the end of any activity which has promoted goodness and truth.

To offer sacrifices in good faith, to serve others for God's glory, and to meditate on God's presence, is Sat. To dedicate every action to God is Sat. But to engage in any sacrifice, to undertake any work, or to attempt meditation, without faith in God, is Asat.

17.23–28

True renunciation

If you renounce every kind of selfish act, then you start on the path of renunciation. If you renounce any prospect of reward for your actions, then you continue on the path of renunciation.

Some sages teach that you should renounce action altogether, since action disturbs meditation. But others say that offering sacrifices and serving others should not be renounced. I affirm the second view, that you should continue to offer sacrifices and serve others, because these actions purify the mind. Yet these actions should always be performed without any thought of reward; that is vital.

You should never renounce your duties; to renounce your duties would be to plunge into darkness. You should never renounce particular actions for fear of difficulties and hardships; that would be sterile. You should fulfil your duties without anxiety or fear; that is true renunciation.

So long as you have a body, you cannot renounce action altogether. True renunciation consists in giving up all desire for personal rewards. Those who are attached to personal rewards, will reap the consequences of their actions; some rewards will be pleasant, some will be painful, and some will be mixed. But those who renounce all desire for personal rewards, will reap no consequences of their actions; they transcend the process of cause and effect.

18.2–12

Thought and action

There are five factors which lie behind all thought and action. These are the body, the sense of self, the means of perception, the performance of the act, and fate. These five factors are present in right thoughts and wrong thoughts, and in good deeds and bad deeds. Those who hold the soul responsible for thought and action, are mistaken; their minds are clouded by folly.

There is thought, the thinker, and thinking itself. There is action, the one who acts, and the act itself. These can be analyzed according to the three forces which bind the body to the soul: peace, assertion and passivity. Thought rooted in peace discerns the indestructible soul in all living beings, and hence perceives the unity within the diversity of existence. Thought rooted in assertion regards every living being and material object as separate and distinct. Thought rooted in passivity perceives one small part of existence, and mistakes it for the whole.

Action rooted in peace is performed from a sense of duty, without thought of personal reward, and without concern whether the task is pleasant or unpleasant. Action rooted in assertion is performed from personal desire, and is liable to cause harm as well as good. Action rooted in passivity is undertaken blindly, without considering the consequences.

18.13–25

Types of intellect and will

There are three types of intellect and will. These correspond to the three forces which bind the body to the soul: peace, assertion and passivity.

The intellect rooted in peace knows when to act, and when to refrain from action; it knows the distinction between right and wrong; it knows the difference between courage and fear, and knows the causes of both; and it knows what brings freedom, and what brings bondage. The intellect rooted in assertion confuses right and wrong; and it cannot distinguish what should be done, from what should not be done. The intellect rooted in passivity is utterly distorted; it regards right as wrong, and wrong as right.

The will rooted in peace keeps the senses and the mind in harmony. The will rooted in assertion pursues wealth, pleasure and social status. The will rooted in passivity is obstinate, lazy, self-pitying, depressed and conceited.

18.29–35

Types of happiness

There are three types of happiness. These correspond to the three forces which bind the body to the soul: peace, assertion, and passivity.

First there is the happiness that comes from always doing what is right. This leads to the end of all sorrow. It may at first seem like bitter poison; but eventually it turns out to be the wine of eternal sweetness. This type of happiness is pure; and it arises from peace.

Secondly there is the happiness which comes from the pleasures of the senses. At first this seems like sweet wine; but eventually it turns out to be bitter poison. This type of happiness arises from assertion.

Thirdly there is the happiness that comes from the pleasures of sleep, indolence and intoxication. From beginning to end this happiness is delusion. It arises from passivity.

18.36–41

Devotion to duty

The qualities which a priest should cultivate are tranquillity, purity of mind, and simplicity of bodily tastes; readiness to forgive, and eagerness to give help; clarity of vision and strength of faith.

The qualities which a warrior should cultivate are a heroic mind and a fiery heart; courage in battle, magnanimity in victory, and fortitude in defeat; and nobility and dignity in leadership.

The qualities which an artisan should cultivate are diligence and skill. And the quality which a labourer should cultivate is willingness to serve.

By devotion to their duty, all people can attain perfection. When people do the work allotted to them to the best of their abilities, they worship the divine Creator who dwells within them.

It is better to perform your own duties imperfectly, than to undertake another person's duties. By doing the work to which you are born, you will never fall into sin.

You should not abandon a particular task because you cannot do it perfectly. Every action is surrounded by defects, just as every fire is surrounded by smoke.

18.42–48

The perfect person

When you have attained perfection, you will have a clear vision of truth. You will be the master of your senses and passions. You will be free from the clamour of likes and dislikes. You will relish the silence of solitude. You will have perfect control of your thoughts and speech. You will want only the simplest food. You will have no feelings of aggression or anger, arrogance or lust. You will be at peace with yourself and with others.

You will be united with me, and so you will be beyond the reach of desire and sorrow. You will love me and know me as I am; you will know my glory, and so enter my boundless being. You will do nothing except in my service; and through me you will win eternal life.

Do you wish to attain perfection? Then make every act an offering to me. Look upon me as your only protector. Meditate upon me constantly. When you face problems, rely on me to overcome them. Strive to follow my will, and not your own.

Remember, I dwell in the hearts of all living beings – including your heart. And I surround all living beings – including you.

18.51–58, 61

The yoga of knowledge, as defined by the *Bhagavad Gita*, requires the practice of meditation. And the supreme instruction of meditation is the *Yoga Sutra*, written by Patanjali in about the third century BCE.

The Hindu view of social order is expressed most clearly in the laws of Manu. These laws were formulated in around the second century BCE, and attributed to a mythical figure who appears in the *Vedas* – Manu simply means 'man'. Their main concern is to delineate the caste system; but their wider significance lies in their description of the four stages of human life – and the varying importance of knowledge and action at each stage.

The most austere of all Hindu sects are the Jains. The founder was Mahavir, who lived in the sixth century BCE; but the greatest expression of their philosophy was by Umasvati, who lived eight hundred years later.

The laws of Manu inspired the composition in south India of the *Kural*, a collection of moral aphorisms. Thus it defines most closely the yoga of action. Its author was called Valluvar, whose name suggests he was a weaver; and he probably lived around the fifth century CE.

By common consent the greatest Hindu philosopher is Sankara, who lived in the eighth century CE. His greatest work is a commentary on the Upanishads; and his interpretation has remained dominant.

The purpose of yoga

Let us explain yoga. It is concerned with freedom from spiritual disturbance. Through yoga the soul becomes perfectly tranquil and serene; without yoga the soul is constantly subject to disturbance.

There are five kinds of disturbance to the soul – some of which are pleasurable, and some painful. The first kind of disturbance is information from the senses. The second is curiosity – the desire to acquire information through the senses. The third consists in concepts, theories and ideals which engender enthusiasm and passion. The fourth is depression. The fifth is memory, which creates the illusion that external objects are permanent.

Patanjali 1.1–6

Five kinds of disturbance

Let us define the five kinds of disturbance more closely.

Information from the senses has three aspects: direct perception of objects through the senses; thinking about those objects, and drawing conclusions about them; and learning about objects from other people.

Curiosity arises from the false belief that knowledge of external objects is true knowledge.

Concepts, theories and ideals engender goals which are false – which do not lead to freedom from disturbance.

Depression arises from the acceptance of evil as genuine and permanent, and hence the conviction that freedom from evil is impossible.

Memory turns perceptions of transient events and objects into permanent figments of the mind. In this way it causes people to confuse transience with permanence.

Patanjali 1.7–11

Effort and patience

Liberation from spiritual disturbance requires both effort and patience.

By effort is meant the practice of the disciplines which yoga specifies. This practice must be continuous; and continuity can only be sustained through great devotion to the ultimate goal – which is perfect serenity.

By patience is meant the willingness to relinquish, one by one, the desires for external objects – both objects which are seen, and objects which are heard. This leads to an acceptance of one's fate, whatever it might be.

Patanjali 1.12–16

Normal and superior consciousness

There are two kinds of consciousness.

First there is normal consciousness. This is where there is a distinction between the subject and the object; the subject is the one who is conscious, the object is the focus of consciousness. Thus normal consciousness is concerned with investigating objects, discriminating between one object and another, and enjoying objects. Normal consciousness is also capable of making itself the object of consciousness.

Secondly there is superior consciousness. Consciousness passes through various stages, gradually freeing itself from the objects of consciousness. Finally consciousness alone remains; this is superior consciousness – which is perfect knowledge.

Patanjali 1.17–18

Commitment to God

Some people inherit from previous lives the ability to attain superior consciousness with little effort. Others can only attain superior consciousness through great faith, exertion, learning, steadiness of mind, and reflection.

Attainment is quickest for those who are most intense in their efforts. Attainment is less quick for those who are moderate in their efforts. Attainment is slowest for those who are mild in their efforts.

Attainment depends on total commitment to God. By God we mean that entity who is unmoved by desire, untouched by misery, and unaffected by action. In God ultimate and infinite knowledge is complete. God is the teacher of teachers, the example to examples. Since he is beyond time, God has existed and will exist at all times.

God is manifest in the syllable Aum. Repeating the syllable Aum, and comprehending its significance, is an aid towards the attainment of superior consciousness.

Patanjali 1.19–28

Inner obstacles

The first step in yoga is to engage in introspection, and thereby understand the inner obstacles that must be overcome.

These obstacles include emotional imbalance, mental laziness, doubt, lack of enthusiasm, lethargy, attachment to pleasures of the senses, delusion, difficulty in sustaining concentration, and susceptibility to distractions.

The symptoms of these inner obstacles are listlessness, depression, inability to relax, and irregular breathing.

The inner obstacles can only be overcome with single-minded and wholehearted effort.

Patanjali 1.29–32

Steadiness of mind

All things conducive to steadiness of mind assist in over-
coming the inner obstacles. Friendship, goodwill towards
other living beings, and indifference to both pleasure and
pain, are conducive to steadiness of mind.

Just as anxious, irregular breathing is a sign of inner
obstacles, so calm, regular breathing helps to overcome those
obstacles.

There are various methods of learning to hold the mind
steady. One method is to become aware of your own awareness of sensory objects – to focus your attention on the senses
themselves, rather than on the objects of the senses. Another
method is to focus your eyes on a source of light. Another
method is to hold your attention steady during a dream, or
in that state between waking and sleeping. Another method
is to fix your attention on some particular external object.

Through learning to hold the mind steady in this manner,
you develop an unobstructed vision of both infinite smallness
and infinite largeness.

                                        Patanjali 1.33–40

The veil covering the soul

Having learned to hold the mind steady, you must learn to distinguish between the soul and that which is not the soul. This implies distinguishing between consciousness, which belongs to the soul, and the sensory objects of consciousness, which do not belong to the soul. Just as it is hard to distinguish a crystal from the colours which suffuse it, so it is hard to distinguish consciousness from its objects.

The soul is covered by three veils. The first veil consists of words; the second veil consists of the meaning of words; and the third veil consists of the ideas attached to those meanings. In order to discern the soul, these veils must be lifted.

When the third veil is lifted, the other two veils fall away. Lifting the third veil requires awareness of the distinction between ideas themselves, and that to which they refer. Consciousness has ideas – and consciousness is permanent. But that to which ideas refer is external to consciousness – and therefore is transient.

This distinction between ideas and that to which they refer, should start with material objects such as a table or a rock; you distinguish between the idea of the object, and the object itself. Then the distinction should proceed to more subtle objects – of which the most subtle is potential energy.

Patanjali 1.41–45

Transcending goals

You practise yoga because you have a goal: you are seeking knowledge of ultimate truth. Yet ultimate truth transcends goals.

When you have attained superior consciousness, you are entirely free from all goals and ambitions; you no longer desire results. Thus the true nature of all existence becomes clear; your consciousness is filled with truth.

Normal consciousness is concerned with the perceptions of the senses, with inferences from what the senses have perceived, and with information provided by other people. Thus normal consciousness consists of knowledge of particular things. Superior consciousness is concerned with the direct intuition of all things as they truly are. Thus superior consciousness transcends perceptions of the senses, inferences and information; it consists of knowledge of existence itself.

When you have attained superior consciousness, you lose all desire for knowledge of particular things. The bliss of superior consciousness obliterates every lower pleasure. Yet in order to know ultimate truth, you must give up this bliss.

Patanjali 1.46–51

The five hindrances

To begin practising yoga you must learn to control your bodily desires; you must learn to watch over yourself; and you must commit yourself without reserve to attaining perfect knowledge of the soul.

The purpose of yoga is to weaken the hindrances which obstruct knowledge of the soul. There are five hindrances: ignorance, egoism, attachment, aversion, and tenacity.

Ignorance is the soil in which the other hindrances grow. It consists in mistaking the transient for the permanent, the impure for the pure, the evil for the good, and the apparent soul for the real soul.

Egoism consists in confusing consciousness with the objects of consciousness – in confusing the one who sees, with that which is seen.

Attachment consists in attraction to sources of pleasure.

Aversion consists in revulsion from sources of pain.

Tenacity consists in the will to stay alive. This is an instinct, which remains strong even in the wise.

These hindrances can only be counteracted by great effort against them. And by meditation their effects can be nullified.

Patanjali 2.1–11

Action leading to sorrow

The principle by which actions have effects, has its root in the hindrances; and it operates continuously, regardless of whether it is felt or not felt. Owing to this principle your actions affect your role in life, the length of your life, and the joys and sorrows which you experience in the course of life. Joy is the fruit of good actions, and sorrow is the fruit of bad actions.

The discriminating mind, however, realizes that sorrow is the effect of all actions. In the case of bad actions sorrow is the direct effect. In the case of good actions sorrow is the indirect effect for two reasons. First there is anticipation that the joy will soon cease – and this anticipation brings sorrow. Secondly there is the grief when the joy actually ceases.

Nonetheless future sorrow can be avoided.

Patanjali 2.12–16

Bondage and release

The ultimate reason for all that is bad and evil is that the soul is bound to the body. The three forces which bind the soul to the body are peace, assertion and passivity. These forces are made manifest both through the organs of the body, and through the elements from which the body is made. Yet, although these forces bind the soul to the body, they can also be redirected in such a manner that they release the soul from the body.

The three forces exist in four states. In the first state they are merely energy. In the second state they possess the capacity to be aware of things. In the third state they have the senses of hearing, touch, sight, taste and smell; they also have a sense of personal identity. In the highest state they are self-aware.

The soul, which is pure consciousness, becomes aware of the body and the external world through the three forces which bind it to the body. All experience comes through this awareness.

Liberation of the soul consists in the three forces releasing the soul from the body; and then all experience ceases. But while the soul is bound to the body, the soul believes it has a body, and the body believes it has a soul.

Patanjali 2.17–23

Seven features of knowledge

The soul's belief that it has a body, and the body's belief that it has a soul, are delusions. When these delusions disappear, the association of the soul with the body ceases. By this means the soul is liberated from the body; and thereafter the soul is utterly free. The way to destroy these delusions is through unfaltering discernment, by which perfect knowledge is acquired.

This knowledge has seven features. The first is omniscience. The second is perfect serenity, in which there are no disturbances. The third is the fusion of subject and object – of consciousness and the objects of consciousness. The fourth is that feelings of duty – all feelings of work that needs to be done – has vanished. The fifth is that the mind has no power over the soul. The sixth is that the three forces which bind the body to the soul – peace, assertion, and passivity – have no power over the mind. And the seventh is that the mind understands the freedom of the soul.

Patanjali 2.24–27

Seven steps of yogic practice

In order to attain perfect knowledge, you must climb up the seven steps of yogic practice. The seven steps are abstinence, cultivation, correct posture, correct breathing, control of the senses, concentration, meditation, and integration.

Abstinence has five aspects. The first is abstaining from violence. The second is abstaining from falsehood. The third is abstaining from theft. The fourth is abstaining from sexual immorality. And the fifth is abstaining from avarice. These five aspects of abstinence are universal, and must be practised regardless of time, place and circumstances.

Cultivation has five aspects. The first is purity. The second is serenity. The third is austerity. The fourth is study. And the fifth is worship of God.

Patanjali 2.28–32

Overcoming evil

Abstinence and cultivation are closely linked, since for each evil requiring abstinence, there is its opposite which should be cultivated.

It is not only wrong to engage in acts of violence yourself; it is wrong to encourage or approve of others doing so. It is not only wrong to utter falsehoods yourself; it is wrong to encourage or approve of others doing so. It is not only wrong to engage in theft yourself; it is wrong to encourage or approve of others doing so. It is not only wrong to engage in sexually immoral acts yourself; it is wrong to encourage or approve of others doing so. It is not only wrong to act avariciously yourself; it is wrong to encourage or approve of others doing so.

When considering how you may cultivate the opposite of any evil within yourself, you should consider the motivation for that evil – whether you are motivated by anger or ignorance. You should consider whether the evil is slight, moderate, or large. And you should consider the kind of misery which results from the evil.

Patanjali 2.33–34

The benefits of abstinence and cultivation

When you overcome the tendency towards violence, you lose all feelings of enmity towards others. When you overcome the tendency towards falsehood, you lose all feelings of ambition. When you overcome the tendency towards theft, the wealth of others is safe in your hands. When you overcome the tendency towards sexual immorality, you gain great energy. And when you overcome the tendency towards avarice, your capacity for knowledge is greatly increased.

When you cultivate purity, all feelings of vanity disappear; you accept your external appearance as it is. When you cultivate serenity, profound bliss flows through you. When you cultivate austerity, you acquire perfect insight into the nature of the body and its organs. When you cultivate the habit of study, your progress towards perfect knowledge accelerates. When you cultivate worship of God, you attain the goal of perfect knowledge.

Patanjali 2.35–45

Posture, breathing and the senses

The correct posture for yoga is one that enables your body to
be both firm and relaxed. The purpose of the correct posture
is to keep your mind alert and attentive, without effort. Any
tensions in the body upset alertness and attentiveness.

The correct breathing for yoga is regular and calm. Breathing may be disturbed by external discomforts, or by discomforts within the body. The length or shortness of each breath
does not matter, and will vary according to time and place.
Breathing may also be disturbed by mental anxieties. Strive to
rid yourself of these disturbances; and if you cannot do so,
strive to ignore them. The purpose of correct breathing is to
keep your mind alert and attentive, without effort.

Control of the senses requires you to make your senses
unresponsive to stimuli. You should watch over your sense
organs, suppressing every feeling of excitement that comes
from them.

Patanjali 2.46–55

Concentration, meditation and integration

Concentration means holding consciousness steady, in a single position. Meditation means allowing knowledge to flow without interruption through consciousness. Integration occurs when consciousness ceases to regard even itself as an object of consciousness.

When there is concentration, meditation and integration, there is perfect knowledge; there is complete unity of consciousness, which is the soul, with God. The soul transcends time and place, and enters eternity and infinity. Those who have mastered the practice of yoga, may enter this state of perfect unity whenever they wish.

The first five steps of yogic practice – abstinence, cultivation, correct posture, correct breathing, and control of the senses – have no value in themselves. Their value consists in their being the preparation for these final three steps. You cannot climb these final three steps without initially climbing the first five steps.

Patanjali 3. 1–8

Disturbance and quietness

The desire to suppress disturbances is itself a disturbance; and it too must be suppressed, in order to liberate yourself from all desire. As you succeed in suppressing all desire, so you become accustomed to the state of being undisturbed; lack of disturbance becomes habitual.

Gradually you cease to distinguish one thing from another; you are simply aware of the unity of all things. You come to realize that the particular traits and features of external objects are manifestations of their fundamental oneness.

Progress in yoga is not straight. After great effort you will enjoy periods of quietness, when you are free of disturbance; and then there will be disturbances again. Do not be anxious about this; this is how spiritual development occurs. The periods of quietness grow longer, and the periods of disturbance grow shorter.

Patanjali 3.9−15

Signs of perfect knowledge

As you attain perfect knowledge, you transcend time; past and future are apprehended as one.

As you attain perfect knowledge, you transcend concepts; words, their meanings, and the ideas they convey, are apprehended as one.

As you attain perfect knowledge, you comprehend fully your previous spiritual condition. Whereas normal consciousness does not understand superior consciousness, superior consciousness understands normal consciousness.

As you attain perfect knowledge, you know fully the spiritual condition of others. But you do not know the content of their minds, because you are indifferent to this.

As you attain perfect knowledge, you cease to be aware of the form of external things. When light does not reach the eye, nothing is visible; in the same way, when the senses do not respond to external stimuli, nothing is sensed.

As you attain perfect knowledge, all actions are intended. When normal consciousness prevails, some actions are intended, while others are unintended. When you reach superior consciousness, this distinction disappears, because you understand fully what you do.

Patanjali 3.16–21

Surrendering attachments, powers and techniques

When you begin to practise yoga, you strive to be friendly towards all people; you show goodwill to all living beings; and you try to become indifferent to pleasure and pain. All this is necessary in order to acquire peace of mind, and thereby overcome the inner obstacles to progress. But as you make progress, you must recognize that even friendliness, goodwill and indifference are attachments; and, along with all other attachments, they must be surrendered.

When you begin to practise yoga, you acquire various powers. These are signs of success. But as you make progress, you must surrender all forms of power.

When you begin to practise yoga, you focus your attention on the senses themselves, rather than on the objects of the sense; or you focus your eyes on a source of light. These are methods of holding the mind steady. But as you make progress, you must dispense with all spiritual methods; you must surrender every technique on which you depend.

Patanjali 3.23–25

Perfecting the mind

By meditating on all living beings on earth, you apprehend the unity of all life.

By meditating on the sun, you apprehend the oneness of all space. By meditating on the moon, you apprehend the timelessness of the stars. By meditating on the polar star, you apprehend the pattern of all the stars.

By meditating on the navel, you apprehend all the organs of the body. By meditating on the throat, you apprehend the cessation of hunger and thirst. By meditating on the eyelids, you apprehend motion and motionlessness.

By meditating on the light within your head, you apprehend the nature of knowledge. By meditating on your intuition, you apprehend how all things are apprehended. By meditating on consciousness, you apprehend God.

Normal consciousness does not distinguish between the mind and the soul. Superior consciousness apprehends the distinction. Yoga makes the mind perfect for the purpose of liberating the soul.

Patanjali 3.25–35

Sublime identity

When you have attained perfect knowledge, you realize that
the senses are not a source of knowledge. The information
which is acquired though hearing, touching, seeing, tasting
and smelling, adds nothing to true knowledge. On the contrary, the sense organs are obstacles to be overcome in attaining perfect knowledge – or, rather, the mind must become
independent of them.

When the soul comes to understand how it is bound to
the body, and loosens the bonds, it also understands the same
bondage in other living beings. Moreover the soul becomes
indifferent to such things as cold, dirt and physical injury.

Through attaining perfect knowledge, you perceive the
sublime identity in variety, the sublime unity in diversity.
You make no distinction between sound and hearing; you
have soundless hearing. You make no distinction between
space and weight; you regard a rock and a feather as the
same. You make no distinction between disturbances and
peace; you understand all disturbances, and so transcend
them. You make no distinction between objects and the elements of which they are comprised. You make no distinction
between objects according to their size and function. To you
all things are as beautiful as the most beautiful flower, because beauty is no longer a matter of the senses.

Superior consciousness does not know God; it is God. It
is not aware of anything; it is awareness.

Patanjali 3.36–49

Entering eternity and infinity

To attain perfect knowledge you must become indifferent to perfect knowledge. The desire for perfect knowledge is the last obstacle that must be overcome, before the soul is utterly liberated.

Those who have only normal consciousness, feel inferior to those with superior consciousness, and so they admire them. But those who aspire to superior consciousness, must know that they will not feel superior to those with normal consciousness. Superior consciousness excludes all feelings of success and status.

To attain perfect knowledge you must become indifferent to time; you should discern eternity in every moment; and you should discern every moment in eternity. And you must become indifferent to space; you should discern infinity in every point, and you should discern every point in infinity.

At the moment when you transcend time, you enter eternity. And at the place where you transcend space, you enter infinity.

When you enter eternity and infinity, you are completely isolated, and utterly at one.

Patanjali 3.50–55

Success in yoga

You may achieve success in yoga through innate ability, through the correct diet, through study, through austerity, and through determination. And by these means you evolve to the highest state of which human beings are capable.

God does not compel or induce you to practise yoga; he exerts no effort on your behalf. You are free to practise yoga, or not to practise yoga, as you wish; and success depends entirely on your own efforts.

Your mind has many interests; but it remains one mind. When you practise yoga, all these diverse interests are unified.

The practice of yoga does not earn merit, nor does it lose merit; in itself it is morally neutral. But by practising yoga you become progressively more inclined to act in a manner that has benign results, and less inclined to act in a manner that has malign results.

Patanjali 4.1—8

Constancy through change

The law of cause and effect cannot be suspended or interrupted; it operates at all times and in all places. Desires motivate actions, and actions have results; the past leads to the present, and the present leads to the future. Sometimes the consequences of actions are visible, and sometimes they are hidden.

The substance of any object is that which remains constant through change. Different minds may observe an object; but the substance of the object does not depend on the minds observing it. An object may be known or unknown, depending on whether a mind perceives it.

The substance of every object is the soul; the soul alone can be altered by the law of cause and effect. The activities of the soul are always known, because the soul knows itself. The soul does not require external illumination, because the soul is its own light. The soul does not know itself, as a mind knows an object; there cannot be consciousness of consciousness, as this would imply consciousness of consciousness of consciousness – and so on, without limit. In the soul subject and object are one. The objects of the soul's consciousness are all things that are not the soul.

Patanjali 4.9–23

The last moment

Those lacking knowledge identify the mind with the soul; but as you grow in knowledge, you discern that the soul is distinct from the mind. Thus you isolate the soul from the mind.

The mind is constantly buffeted by desires and other disturbances; this is because the mind is part of the body. By isolating the soul from the mind, the soul is liberated from the body. Thus the soul is free from all disturbance; it is no longer tied to the law of cause and effect. And this freedom is perfect knowledge.

When the mind is isolated from the soul, the three forces which bind the soul to the body – peace, assertion, and passivity – lose their power. The last moment in which the soul is identified with the mind, is the last moment in which these forces operate. In the next moment the soul, which is pure consciousness, is utterly pure; that next moment is eternal. Aum.

Patanjali 4.24–34

The student's life

The student of truth should wear whatever clothes his teacher prescribes. If his teacher tells him to wear the skin of a particular animal, the student should obtain a robe made from that skin. If the teacher tells him to wear a particular style of belt, or to carry a staff made from the wood of a particular tree, the student should do so.

The student should not eat honey or meat; and he should not eat dairy products that have been allowed to turn. He should not put perfume on his body, nor should he wear garlands or any kind of adornment. He should avoid causing injury to any living being. If he feels anger or greed surging within him, he should suppress it. He should not dance or sing or play musical instruments for amusement. He should not gamble or indulge in idle gossip; he should avoid disputes, and he should never tell lies.

He should not look at a woman with eyes of lust, and he should never touch a woman. He should sleep alone, and strive to avoid shedding his semen.

He should beg for food each morning. He should beg only from families who are devout in performing religious rituals. But if there are not enough devout families, he may beg from any family. He should never confine his begging to a single family.

Manu 2.174, 177–180, 182–183, 185, 188

The student and the teacher

The student should always eat inferior food to that of his teacher, and wear inferior clothes. He should rise from his bed earlier, and go to his bed later. When he speaks to his teacher, he should stand and face his teacher; he should never speak while he is eating. When he sees his teacher approaching, he should rise to his feet and walk towards him. If he meets his teacher on sloping ground, he should stand on the lower place. When his teacher is instructing him, he should ensure that his seat is lower than that of his teacher.

He should never mock his teacher by imitating his gait, his speech or his movements. If he hears people speaking ill of his teacher, or reproaching his teacher, he should put his hands over his ears and go away.

The student who speaks ill of his teacher, will become a donkey in his next life. The student who reproaches his teacher, will become a dog. The student who lives off his teacher, eating food that has been given to his teacher, will become a worm. The student who is grudging towards his teacher, will become a bug.

The student should never say anything that he would not be happy for his teacher to hear. If the teacher's teacher appears, the student should treat him like his own teacher. The student should never meet members of his own family without his teacher's permission.

Manu 2.194–197, 199–201, 203, 205

Learning from all people

Just as a man digging with a spade eventually finds water, so the student listening to his teacher eventually finds truth.

A student should observe the behaviour of all people. If a student observes some man or woman whose conduct is especially fine, he should strive to imitate that conduct. Even the lowliest person can be a worthy example.

The student should regard his teacher as the embodiment of ultimate truth. He should regard his father as the embodiment of the spirit who created the universe. He should regard his mother as the embodiment of the spirit of the earth. He should treat them all with profound respect. The effort which his parents have expended in raising him, can never be repaid, even in a hundred years. Thus he should always strive to please them, as well as his teacher. When all three are satisfied with him, then he can feel satisfied with himself. He should do nothing without their approval.

When the student has learnt to respect his teacher and his parents, then he will find it easy to respect all other men and women. He should seek wisdom from every person he meets. Just as ambrosia can be extracted from poison, and gold can be found in a lump of clay, so spiritual insights can be heard in the mouth of a child, and wise advice can be uttered by an enemy.

Manu 2.218, 223, 225–228, 239

Becoming a householder

When a young man is familiar with the sacred texts, and has learnt to live in accordance with their precepts, he should become a householder. He should marry a woman whose attitudes and values are in harmony with his own. In choosing a suitable wife, he should not be swayed by sexual desire.

He should have sexual intercourse with his wife during her fertile period, so she will bear children. He should never seek sexual satisfaction apart from with his wife.

A householder has many material concerns. Nonetheless he should devote a period of each day to the study of the sacred texts, reminding himself of what he learnt as a student. He should also be diligent in performing the religious rituals which the sacred texts prescribe.

Just as all living beings depend on the air, so people in the other stages of life depend on the householder; he provides the food which they eat and the clothes which they wear. Therefore people in the other stages of life should treat the householder with respect. By performing his duties with diligence, the householder earns for himself great merit – which will bring happiness in future lives.

Manu 3.1–4, 45, 75, 77–79

The householder's work

The first quarter of a man's life should be spent as a student, living with a teacher; and the second quarter should be spent as a householder, living with a wife.

He should earn his living by a profession which does no harm, or very little harm, to other living beings. Only in extreme circumstances – when his own survival, or that of his family requires it – is it permissible to injure other living beings.

He may accumulate some wealth through his work, so long as he does nothing which is improper and dishonest. But he should not work so hard that he causes stress to his body or mind. It is better for him to live simply, subsisting on the bare necessities, than to ruin his health in becoming rich.

If a man cannot find normal work, he may feed himself and his family by gathering the grains which are dropped on the ground at harvest. This is quite lawful – and is far preferable to engaging in some trade which exploits others.

He should never become addicted to any particular pleasure, nor should he become attached to any particular object. And he should renounce any activity that distracts him from studying the sacred texts each day.

He should not pretend to be richer or younger than he is. His clothes should reflect his level of wealth and his age.

Manu 4.1–5, 11, 16–18

Living in the forest

After a man has lived as a householder for a quarter of his life, he should retreat into the forest, in order to restrain and master his senses. The time to do this is when his skin has become wrinkled, his hair is turning grey, and his children have themselves produced children. He should invite his wife to come with him into the forest; but if she does not wish to come, he should entrust her to his sons.

He should renounce all kinds of cultivated food, and eat only what the forest provides. Thus he should gather the vegetables and grains that grow naturally beneath the trees, and he should pick the fruits and nuts that grow on the trees. He should not eat honey; nor should he consume any leaves that might affect his mind. He may cook what he has gathered; and he may make a simple pestle and mortar to grind up the grains. Even if he is suffering extreme hunger, he should not go to a village for food; he should not even eat what village people have thrown out.

In the seasons when food is abundant in the forest, he should gather large amounts, and store it; in this way he will have ample time for spiritual reflection in the seasons when food is scarce. He may eat his food at any time of the day he wishes.

Through the day he should vary his posture. Sometimes he should lie down, sometimes sit, and sometimes stand up. He should wash his body regularly. In the cold season he should often wear wet clothes; this will increase his inner warmth.

                                   Manu 6.1–3, 13–14, 16–17, 19, 22–23

Becoming a wandering ascetic

When a man has spent the third quarter of his life as a forest-dweller, he should abandon all attachments, and spend the final quarter of his life wandering from place to place as an ascetic. A person who has spent the first quarter his life studying the sacred texts, the second quarter as a householder, the third quarter as a forest-dweller mastering his senses, and the fourth quarter as a wandering ascetic, will thrive after death.

The life of the student, the householder, and the forest-dweller, may be regarded as the repayment of debts. Once the repayment is complete, a man is truly free – and therefore is capable of becoming a wandering ascetic. But a man who has not repaid these debts, is not free – and therefore is not ready to become a wandering ascetic.

The wandering ascetic should always travel alone, without a companion. In this way he can neither desert anyone nor be deserted by anyone; and this will help to ensure success. He should have no home and no hearth. To obtain food he should go into a village each day. But he should be indifferent as to what food is given to him. And he should not engage in conversation; rather he should remain in deep meditation. His only possessions should be a bowl made from the skull of an animal, and a few rags to cover his body.

Manu 6.33–35, 42–44

The ascetic's life

The wandering ascetic should not welcome death, nor should he fear death; he should wait for death as a servant waits for orders. If he is ever required to speak, his words should be purified by the truth. He should endure insults with equanimity, and he should despise no one; he should regard everyone as a friend. He should not respond to anger with anger; but when people curse or threaten him, he should bless them. He should not respond to lies with lies, but always speak honestly. He should suppress every bodily desire. He should regard the soul as his only companion, and bliss as his only goal.

He should never try to obtain food by interpreting portents and omens, nor by reading the stars or people's palms. He should never beg from a family whose house is already swarming with beggars. He should keep his hair and beard neatly trimmed, and his nails cut, so that his appearance does not frighten people. He should keep his bowl clean.

He should go begging only once a day; and when he has obtained enough food for survival, he should stop begging. If he allows himself to become addicted to large amounts of food, he will soon be addicted to many other sensory objects also. He should only beg from a family when they have finished their meal, asking merely for what has been left. He should never grovel for food, but take only what is given with goodwill.

Manu 6.45–48, 50–52, 55–56, 58

The ascetic's freedom

The ascetic should strive not to harm any living creature. Before he drinks, he should strain the water, so that he does not accidentally consume some tiny insect. And when he walks, he should constantly inspect the ground ahead of him, so that he does not tread on an insect or reptile. He should also bathe frequently, to wash away any insects that may have lodged on his body; and he should beware of breathing in any insects.

He should frequently repeat the sacred syllable Aum. He should meditate frequently on the destiny of living beings: that those whose lives are good, are reborn to a higher state; and that those whose lives are bad, are reborn to a lower state. As he comes to understand at the deepest level this process of cause and effect, he will break free from it; but while he does not fully understand it, he remains bound to the cycle of birth and death.

When he finally dies, his soul will abandon his body as a bird flies from a tree. He will cast the credit for his good deeds on those who have respected him; and he will cast the discredit for his bad deeds on those who have despised him. He himself will attain the ultimate truth.

Manu 6.67–69

Categories of truth

The path to liberation consists in having an enlightened world-view, in possessing enlightened knowledge, and in behaving in an enlightened manner.

Having an enlightened world-view consists in accepting the categories of truth as they are. This may arise spontaneously, or through learning.

There are seven categories of truth. There is the soul, which is sentient. There are objects, which are non-sentient. There are effects on the soul. There are ways these effects bind themselves to the soul. There is obstruction of these effects. There is reduction of these effects. And there is liberation from these effects.

These categories can be analyzed according to their potentiality, and according to their actuality. They can be understood through studying sacred texts, and through philosophical reflection. They can be observed to determine cause and duration. And they can be listed according to number and place.

Umasvati 1.1–8

Types of knowledge

There are five types of knowledge. There is empirical knowledge, which is knowledge gained from observation and experience. There is verbal knowledge, which is knowledge conveyed through words. There is clairvoyance, which is knowledge beyond the perception of the senses. There is telepathy, which is direct knowledge of the mind of another person. And there is omniscience.

The first two types of knowledge are acquired in the normal course of life. The other three types of knowledge are gained through spiritual discipline.

Empirical knowledge depends on sorting out the images and impressions which the senses receive. This involves memory, recognition, and reason. Thus empirical knowledge is gained through the combination of the senses and the mind. Verbal knowledge follows in the wake of empirical knowledge.

Clairvoyance occurs when the individual obstructs and reduces the effects of external activity on the soul. Mind-reading occurs when the effects of external activity are eliminated altogether.

Umasvati 1.9−14, 20, 23, 26

Classes of being

The essence of any being is to be worthy of liberation, or unworthy of liberation. The beings unworthy of liberation are worldly; they move from one life to another. The beings worthy of liberation are unwordly; they break free from the cycle of birth and rebirth.

Worldly beings fall into two categories: those that are mobile, and those that are immobile. Immobile beings have bodies with only one sense. Mobile beings have bodies with two or more senses.

Bodies made of minerals, such as clay and metal, have only one sense; so also do bodies made of water, such as snow, ice and rain; so also do bodies made of vegetable, such as plants and trees. The sense which all these bodies possess is the sense of touch.

Worms, ants, bees and the like have two senses: touch and taste. Ants, fleas, lice, termites and centipedes, have three senses: touch, taste and smell. Wasps, flies, gnats, butterflies, moths and scorpions have four senses: touch, taste, smell and sight. Larger beings such as fish, birds, animals and humans have five senses: touch, taste, smell, sight, and hearing.

Some beings with five senses also have minds, which give them the capacity for rational thought. These include humans and four-legged animals.

Umasvati 2.7, 10, 12−14, 23−25

Types of body

There are five types of living body.

The first is the visible body. It is made from clusters of matter.

The second is the protean body. This is made from a combination of clusters of matter and spiritual powers. This body causes movement in the visible body, and is the location of the will.

The third is the conveyance body. This is the body that accumulates knowledge. It is also the body that conveys the soul from one visible body to another. The ascetic uses this body to practise meditation and to subdue the senses.

The fourth is the fiery body. This is made of particles of fire. It enables the visible body to digest food. In the ascetic, who has learnt to survive on very little food, the fiery body emits hot rays.

The fifth is the effects body. This is the body which receives the effects of good and bad actions. It moves with the soul from one visible body to the next.

Umasvati 2.37

Types of substance

Motion and rest, space and matter, are substances. The soul is also a substance. These substances are eternal, and their number is fixed.

Of these five substances, only matter has the material qualities of touch, taste, smell and colour. The others do not have material qualities.

Of these five substances, motion, rest and space are each a single indivisible whole; they are each one substance. Matter exists in separate clusters throughout the cosmos. And the soul exists as many entities, infinite in number, and incapable of destruction.

The soul can occupy any amount of space; it may be tiny, or it may be vast. Like the light of a lamp, the soul assumes the size of the body it happens to occupy, expanding and contracting as the body expands and contracts.

Matter is the cause of body, speech, mind and breath. Pleasure and pain are also due to matter. And matter determines life and death.

Soul in one being influences the soul in other beings. The soul may exert a benign influence, or a malign influence. The soul in one being can exist independently from other souls.

Umasvati 5.1–5, 15–16, 19–21

Ways of harming the soul

Moving, speaking, and thinking constitute action. Some actions involve just movement; some actions involve just speaking; some actions involve just thinking; some actions involve a combination of two or all three of these. Every action has effects on the soul.

Good actions have beneficial effects on the soul. Evil actions have harmful effects on the soul.

The actions of a person bound by passion bind the soul. The actions of a person free from passion liberate the soul.

There are various gates by which the effects of bad actions reach the soul. There are the five senses: touch, taste, smell, sight, and hearing. There are the four passions: anger, pride, deceit, and greed. And there are the five indulgences: violence, falsehood, theft, sexual immorality, and possessiveness.

The degree to which bad actions affect the soul, depends on three factors. First, the passion with which the action is performed; if the passion is intense, the effects will be greater. Secondly, whether the action is done deliberately or accidentally; a deliberate action has worse effects on the soul than an accidental action. Thirdly, the enthusiasm with which the action is performed; an action performed enthusiastically is worse than an action performed reluctantly.

Umasvati 6. 1–7

Ways of benefiting the soul

There are sixteen gates by which the effects of good actions reach the soul.

There is purity of world-view. This in turn consists of eight factors: absence of suspicion; absence of misguided tendencies; absence of doubt; absence of delusion; strong conviction; firmness of intention; affection for truth; and belief in the supremacy of truth.

There is humility. This means reverence for the path of liberation, and respect for those that guide people onto this path.

There is abstinence. This means abstinence from the four passions of anger, pride, deceit, and greed. And it means abstinence from the five indulgences of violence, falsehood, theft, sexual immorality, and possessiveness.

There is cultivation of knowledge. This means meditating on the seven categories of truth: the soul, which is sentient; objects, which are non-sentient; effects on the soul; the ways these effects bind themselves to the soul; the obstruction of these effects; the reduction of these effects; and liberation from these effects.

There is dread of worldly existence. This means constant anxiety about suffering, which is the central feature of worldly existence.

There is charity. This means sharing your food with ascetics. It also means sharing your knowledge with those with less knowledge than you have.

Umasvati 6.23a

Further ways of benefiting the soul

There is austerity. This means mortifying the body.

There is relating to other people who wish to liberate the soul. Such relationships will only be beneficial if they are peaceful and harmonious.

There is practical service to those who wish to liberate the soul.

There is devotion to those who have attained a high degree of spiritual liberation.

There is devotion to those who teach the way of spiritual liberation.

There is devotion to those who follow the way of spiritual liberation.

There is adherence to those spiritual practices which are vital in attaining spiritual liberation. The first of these practices is daily meditation, during which perfect equanimity is maintained. The second is daily acknowledgement of bad actions in the past. The third is daily reflection on continuing bodily attachments. And the fourth is daily commitment to avoid bad actions in the future.

There is promotion of the way of spiritual liberation. This means preaching about it to others.

And there is the study of sacred texts which describe and analyze the path of spiritual liberation.

Umasvati 6.23b

The five vows

There are five vows: to abstain from violence; to abstain from falsehood; to abstain from theft; to abstain from sexual immorality; and to abstain from avarice.

Householders make vows of partial abstinence; these are called the small vows. Ascetics make vows of complete abstinence; these are called great vows.

Umasvati 7. 1−2

Supporting the five vows

There are five practices which support the vow of abstaining from violence. These are: controlling speech; controlling the mind; moving about with care; handling implements with care; and inspecting food and drink before consuming it.

There are five practices which support the vow of abstaining from falsehood. These are giving up anger; giving up greed; giving up timidity; giving up gossip; and thinking before speaking.

There are five practices which support the vow of abstaining from theft. These are: staying in remote places, such as mountain caves; staying in deserted places, such as ruined houses; staying only with other ascetics; only accepting food which has been freely given; and avoiding disputes with other ascetics about articles in common use.

There are five practices which support the vow of abstaining from sexual immorality. These are: not listening to lewd stories about women; not looking at those parts of the female body which arouse sexual feelings; not recalling past sexual experiences; not eating spicy food; and not decorating or adorning one's own body.

There are five practices which support the vow of abstaining from avarice. These are: taking no pleasure in the sense of touch; taking no pleasure in the sense of taste; taking no pleasure in the sense of smell; taking no pleasure in the sense of sight; and taking no pleasure in the sense of hearing.

Umasvati 7.3–8

Observing the great vows

Breaking the vows causes nothing but suffering, both to the person that breaks them, and to others. By recognizing this, the ascetic is reminded of the importance of keeping the vows.

Those observing the vows should cultivate friendliness towards all living beings. They should show respect for the efforts and accomplishments of others. They should have compassion for any living being who is suffering. And they should be oblivious to people's worldly status.

Those observing the vows should reflect frequently on the lure of worldly ambitions, in order to be frightened of them. And they should reflect on the vanity of worldly achievements, in order to be indifferent to them.

To perform any action out of passion is violent. To speak any untrue word is falsehood. To take anything which has not been given, is theft. To touch another person out of erotic desire is sexual activity. To cling to any object is possession. Those observing the vows should avoid all these thorns.

Umasvati 7.5–12

Observing the small vows

Householders should take and observe the small vows. There are seven practices which enable householders to observe the small vows.

The first is not to travel beyond a limited area. The second is progressively to reduce this area. The third is to treat the natural environment with great care. The fourth is to act with kindness towards all living beings. The fifth is to fast regularly. The sixth is to live simply, constantly striving to use fewer goods. The seventh is to give freely to ascetics.

When householders feel strongly tempted to transgress any of their vows, they should immediately start to fast; and they should continue fasting until the temptation has passed.

When householders become aware that death is approaching, they should fast until they die. This will purge the soul of all passions and impurities, and enable death to be embraced with joy and serenity.

Umasvati 7.15–17

Transgressing the small vows

There are five ways of trangressing each of the five small vows.

These are the five ways of trangressing the vow to abstain from violence: tethering an animal; beating any living being; piercing the skin of any living being; overloading a pack-animal; withholding food and drink from any living being.

These are the five ways of trangressing the vow to abstain from falsehood: giving wrong instruction; divulging secrets; forging documents; misusing funds entrusted to one's care; and disclosing confidential discussions.

These are the five ways of transgressing the vow to abstain from theft: abetting robbery; dealing in stolen goods; evading taxes; misrepresenting the weights of goods one is buying or selling; and dealing in counterfeit goods.

These are the five ways of transgressing the vow to abstain from sexual immorality: looking for opportunities to make sexual liaisons; promiscuity; sex with prostitutes; unnatural sexual practices; and intense sexual passion.

These are the five ways of transgressing the vow to abstain from avarice: inhabiting a house too large for one's needs; striving to increase one's stock of gold and silver; working harder than is necessary to feed one's family; employing servants; acquiring unnecessary furniture.

Umasvati 7.19–24

Fasting and charity

Fasting has six beneficial effects. You will become free of all desire. You will not desire a longer life. You will not desire a shorter life. You will not desire the company of friends. You will not desire any pleasures of the senses. You will not desire approval.

The value of any act of charity is determined by four factors. The first factor is the motivation: if it is motivated by a surge of compassion, the act has only limited value; but if it is motivated by a dispassionate sense of duty, the act has greater value. The second factor is the nature of the gift: if the gift benefits the body of the recipient, the act has only limited value; but if the gift benefits the soul, the act has greater value. The third factor is the state of the giver: if the giver has any ulterior purpose, the act has only limited value; but if the giver has no purpose apart from the good of the recipient, the act has greater value. The fourth factor is the state of the recipient: if the recipient has not taken the five vows, the act has only limited value; but if the recipient has taken the five vows, and observes them, the act has greater value.

Umasvati 7.32, 34

Causes of bondage

There are five causes of spiritual bondage.

The first cause is a deluded world-view. This may come
about through speculation, in which people invent theories
about supernatural phenomena in their minds. It may come
about through blind faith, in which people believe religious
doctrines without understanding them. And it may come
about through undue scepticism, causing people to believe
nothing.

The second cause of bondage is failure to keep the five
vows – of abstinence from violence, from falsehood, from
theft, from sexual immorality, and from possessiveness.

The third cause of bondage is
spiritual laxity, in which the individual keeps the vows, but without enthusiasm.

The fourth cause of bond-
age is passion.

The fifth cause of bond-
age is bad action.

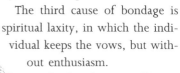

Umasvati 8.1

Attaining omniscience

Omniscience is attained when all delusions are eliminated. This happens when the soul has broken free from the five causes of bondage.

Once omniscience has been attained, it cannot be lost. When the soul has broken free from the five causes of bondage, it cannot again be bound by them. The soul is then liberated for all eternity.

When the soul is omniscient, it has perfect knowledge and perfect intuition. It also has infinite energy and infinite bliss.

The omniscient soul is no longer constrained by the body. Therefore some people have suggested that it expands to the size of the entire universe. But in truth size now becomes irrelevant.

When the soul is liberated, it acquires many powers. It can heal diseases by a touch of the hand. It can subjugate any animal by a look of the eye. It can walk on water, dive into land, and fly through the sky. It can become invisible at will. The senses can operate at a great distance from the object being sensed. And it can read minds.

Umasvati 10.1–2, 4, 7

Knowledge, wisdom and virtue

The acquisition of knowledge is useless – unless it leads to the feet of God. God is pure intelligence. Those who know God, rise above desire and fear; above liking and hating; and even above good and evil. By clasping the feet of God, they are carried across the sea of birth and death.

Every spiritual teacher extols the value of self-denial. Those who renounce all pleasure, shine with joy; those who have mastered their senses, glow with wisdom. Such people can do the impossible.

What better investment exists than the acquisition of virtue? Through acquiring virtue you become both wealthy and indifferent to wealth. Virtue has four opposites: envy, greed, anger and cruelty. Virtue is the perfect companion; on the day you die, you will find virtue to be an undying friend. Do not waste a day in the acquisition of virtue; from virtue alone comes happiness.

Valluvar 2, 4–5, 8, 21, 23–24, 26,
31–32, 35–36, 38–39

Love and family

A good householder is a steadfast friend to ascetics, and to the poor and needy; he willingly offers food to them.

A happy home bears love as its flower, and virtue as its fruit.

A good wife takes pleasure in managing her home well, ensuring that her family lives within her husband's means. With a good wife, what does a man lack? With a bad wife, what good is there in a man's life?

What blessing is greater than bright and healthy children? Sweeter than honey is food messed up with the small hands of a child. More pleasant than the sound of a flute or lute is the sound of a child's lisp. No pleasure is greater than that of a father, when his growing son starts to work at his side.

Those whose hearts are empty of love, seek solace in possessions; those whose hearts are filled with joy, find joy in sharing their possessions. From love of other people comes devotion to God; from devotion to God comes spiritual enlightenment; from spiritual enlightenment comes eternal bliss.

As a worm withers in the sun, so the loveless wither in the warm presence of the loving.

Valluvar 41–42, 45, 51, 53, 61, 64–66,
70, 72, 74–75, 77

Wealth and generosity

There is only one purpose for which a man should acquire wealth beyond the needs of his family: to help others. If he is happy to welcome guests into his house, then he may have a larger house than his family needs.

Never eat a meal alone, when there is someone hungry outside. Those who are generous to others, will themselves receive help at their time of need. Generosity is a seed, which bears a rich harvest. To be wealthy, and yet to give nothing to others, is to suffer poverty of the heart.

Words of truth, which are soaked in love, taste sweet. More precious than the most precious gift are kind words, spoken with a smiling face. Those who are generous in praising others, are praised by all; their words are jewels which everyone admires.

A good deed, which is done not in return for a good deed, nor in the expectation of being returned, can never be repaid. A good deed, performed at the hour of need, is greater than the whole earth.

There is nothing to be gained from gaining wealth by dishonest means. Those who work honestly and live modestly, deserve the highest respect.

Valluvar 81–83, 85, 89, 91–92, 94–95,
101–102, 113, 117

Self-control

Self-control carries you upwards into brightness; lack of self-control takes you downwards into darkness. Guard self-control like a treasure; there is nothing more precious in this life. Those who are able to control themselves, attain great glory.

Guard your tongue, for it is highly dangerous; unguarded words can cause terrible distress. A single bad word can destroy a vast quantity of good. A wound caused by fire will eventually heal; but a wound caused by the tongue leaves a scar that never heals.

Guard your conduct with care; no amount of scholarship is a substitute for good conduct. Class is not a matter of birth, but of conduct; those who behave well deserve the highest place, while those who behave badly should be treated with contempt. Good conduct sows seeds of happiness; bad conduct causes fountains of misery.

Those who cannot control their sexual passions, are utter fools. It is better to die than to commit adultery, because adultery destroys trust and desecrates the home. Adulterers tell themselves that their misconduct is trivial; but they will bring down upon themselves hatred, fear and disgrace.

Valluvar 121–123, 127–129, 131–133, 142–146

Envy, greed and slander

The earth bears the onslaught of the spade and the plough; in the same way you should bear the onslaught of insults. It is good to forgive the sins committed against you; it is better still to forget them. The pleasure of revenge lasts for a day; the joy of forgiveness lasts for eternity. So conquer your enemies with forbearance.

Those who envy the wealth of others, corrupt their own hearts. They are their own worst enemies. Nothing has ever been gained through envy; and nothing has ever been lost through lack of envy.

Excessive desire for wealth destroys the home, and leads to crime. What use is a sharp mind, if it is driven by a greedy heart? Devious schemes for acquiring wealth frequently fail; so those who constantly devise such schemes, are liable to lose whatever wealth they first possessed. Fortune seeks those with wisdom and virtue, not those with avarice.

The person with the worst reputation is the one who ruins the reputation of others; no name is more despised than the slanderer's name. It is better to scoff openly at virtue, than tell lies about virtuous people behind their backs. Slanderers pretend to be righteous; but behind their pose they have evil hearts.

Valluvar 151–152, 155–156, 158, 163, 165, 170,
171, 175–176, 179, 181–182, 185

Words and actions

Empty words, spoken at length, reveal the emptiness of the speaker's mind. Crude words, spoken in public, reveal the corruption of the speaker's mind. Stupid words, spoken by someone who commands respect, undermines that respect. It is sometimes necessary to speak hard and uncomfortable words. But wise people avoid idle speech; and discerning people avoid superficial chatter.

Good people are afraid to strut about in the robes of evil. They fear evil as they fear fire; just as fire can quickly spread from one place to another, so one sin quickly leads to another. The height of wisdom is not to return evil for evil. Avoid committing sin without thinking; the effects of a thoughtless sin are the same as those of a deliberate sin. Do not plead poverty as an excuse for doing wrong; your wrongdoing would make you even poorer. If you wish to avoid sorrow for yourself, avoid causing sorrow to others.

Does a cloud bring rain in the expectation of being rewarded? No; and when you perform your duties, you should have no thought of reward. You should work hard and earn wealth in order to help others. There is no joy on earth greater than the joy of being generous. Treat all your neighbours with the kindness you show to members of your own family. The wealth of a generous person is like a lake that is always full.

Valluvar 191–195, 197–198, 201–206,
211–215

True charity and true wealth

Give to those who are too poor to give anything in return; that is true charity – and every other gift in reality is a form of exchange. It is far better to give than to receive. Do not look for excuses for not giving; look instead for opportunities to give. Feeling pity for someone in need is painful; relieving that need with a gift brings joy to both the receiver and the giver. It is noble to endure hunger; it is almost as noble to relieve hunger. Those who help the poor, lay up true treasure for themselves.

The only asset in this life is a reputation for generosity. The only praise worth hearing is praise for acts of kindness. The fame of a charitable person stands like a tower that can never be destroyed. Charity turns loss into gain, and death into life.

The true wealth of wealthy people consists in the generosity with which they share their wealth with others. When people accumulate wealth, they should accumulate generosity in equal measure. Those who are kind to all living beings, need have no fear for the future. The wind of grief which blows relentlessly across the world, never touches those with generous hearts and hands. Those who are never kind and generous, do not understand the nature of wealth. If everyone in this world were generous, no one would be poor.

Valluvar 221–226, 231–233, 235, 241–242,
244–247

Penance and honesty

Penance consists in bearing your own pain with fortitude, and not causing pain to others. Penance is practised by those whose faith is strong; to others it is pointless. Through penance enemies can be vanquished, and friends supported. Through penance people can obtain what their hearts most deeply desire; whereas those who strive to satisfy their own desires, ultimately obtain nothing. As fire refines gold, so pain refines the hearts of those who treat it as penance. Even death is no obstacle to those strengthened by penance.

There are many people who pretend to be good and holy, yet secretly do evil. They are weaklings posing as giants; they are oxen dressed in tigers' skin; they are hunters hiding behind a bush, ready to pounce on their prey. There is no one so cruel as the person who dresses as an ascetic, and yet lives by deceit. The lute is bent, and the arrow straight; judge people by their acts, not by their looks. There is no need to wear the robes of an ascetic, in order to lead a holy life.

An honest utterance is one without evil intentions or consequences. Even a lie may be honest, if it is intended to do good, and succeeds in doing good. Do not lie against your own conscience, as your conscience will grow hot, and burn your heart; those who always speak in accordance with their consciences, are the true monarchs of this world. Honesty in word and action outweighs even penance and charity.

Valluvar 261–262, 264–267, 269, 272–274, 276, 279–280, 291–295

Anger and murder

No task requires more strength than curbing your own anger; no deed does greater harm than a deed driven by uncurbed anger. Ineffective anger is bad; but effective anger is far worse. Be angry with no one; nothing but evil comes from anger. Do laughter and love have greater enemies than anger? Even if someone is blazing with anger against you, control your own wrath. A mind free of wrath achieves its intentions.

A pure heart never hurts others for the sake of wealth and renown; a pure heart never returns hurt for hurt; and a pure heart never avenges an insult. When people injure or insult you, punish them with a good deed; their shame will be unbearable. Those with pure hearts treat the suffering of others as their own; and they never do to others what would cause harm to themselves.

The greatest virtue is never to kill another living being. Charity is important, and honesty is important; but these count for nothing compared with cherishing life itself. Righteousness may be defined as treating all life as sacred. Ascetics renounce the world, for fear of being reborn into the world; how much better to fear murder and renounce killing! Even at the cost of losing your own life, you should avoid taking another life.

Valluvar 301–304, 308–309, 311–316,
321–325, 327

Transcience and permanence

To mistake the transient for the permanent is foolish and pitiable. Great wealth, like the crowd at a theatrical performance, quickly gathers – and quickly disperses. Wealth never remains; so use it now on that which does remain. Each day is like a knife hacking away at life; do not delay in undertaking good works.

As you renounce the pleasures of life one by one, the pain of life decreases little by little. If you are impatient to attain true joy, then start renouncing pleasure at once; great bliss awaits the ascetic. Control the five senses, and suppress every desire; attachment to objects of the senses is delusion. On the road to spiritual freedom the body itself is a burden; so, if you wish to travel speedily, cast aside the baggage of attachment. The thread of attachment is an endless tangle; cut the thread with the sword of detachment.

To mistake the unreal for the real brings misery and sorrow. The pure vision of the real, unclouded by illusions, brings the radiance of eternal joy. Without the sense of what is real and unreal, the five bodily senses are worthless. The mark of wisdom is to perceive the reality behind every appearance. Those who have seen reality here on earth, will not return to earth after death; when reality has been sought and grasped, rebirth ceases.

Valluvar 331–335, 341–345, 349,
351–352, 354–357

Freedom and destiny

For all living beings at all times, desire is the seed of rebirth. Your only desire should be to break free from the cycle of birth and rebirth; and the only way to fulfil that desire is to have no desires. There is no greater fortune than to be indifferent to fortune; there is no greater happiness than to have no wish for happiness.

Purity consists in being free from desire; and freedom from desire comes from seeking the truth. There is no other freedom than being free from desire; every other kind of freedom is in reality a form of bondage. If you allow desire to surge freely within you, you enslave yourself; if you learn to control desire, you liberate yourself. Where there is no desire, there is no sorrow; as desire ceases to flow, bliss starts to flow.

If you accept your destiny, you will fill yourself with energy; if you resist your destiny, you will drain yourself of energy. Those who resist their destiny, blunt their minds; those who regard their destiny as a friend, sharpen their minds. Do not try to be different from what you are; do not try to obtain what is not naturally yours.

Valluvar 361–366, 368–369, 371–372, 376

Knowledge and ignorance

Learn what should be learnt; and then live according to what you have learnt. Letters and words on a page, if they are written by people of wisdom, will open your eyes. The ignorant are blinded by their ignorance; the educated can see all around them. It is a pleasure to meet and converse with a scholar, and a pain to part. When a well is dug in porous soil, it quickly fills with water; an educated mind quickly fills with wisdom.

To speak to someone who has no desire for knowledge, is like playing dice without a board. It is as hard for a child to pass for an adult, as for an ignorant person to pass for an educated one. Let fools hold their tongues in the presence of the wise. The random facts which fools know, do not comprise genuine knowledge. The self-confidence which fools may exhibit, collapses as soon as discussion starts. The ignorant are like saline soil; they exist, but they are useless.

Through the ear wisdom can be heard; so the ear is the means of acquiring true wealth. Only when the ear's hunger for knowledge has been satisfied, should you satisfy the stomach's hunger for food. You may not be able to read; but so long as you can hear, you can always learn. The wisdom spoken by the wise is like a staff on a slippery path.

Valluvar 391–394, 396, 401–406,
411–412, 414–415

Wisdom and nobility

Wisdom is an inner fortress, which no enemy can raze. It checks the wandering mind, turning it from evil to good. It grasps the truth of whatever is said. It expresses subtle matters with simplicity, and it discerns the subtlety of simple matters. Whereas prudence always flows with the world, wisdom may flow or refuse to flow as it thinks fit. Fools think that the ways of the world are wise; but the wise know where the ways of the world lead.

Nobility consists in being free from arrogance, irritability, and pettiness; it consists in being impartial and unbiased in judgement. People of nobility see the faults of others in proportion; whereas those without nobility mistake a millet of fault for a melon.

Seek out those who are wise and noble, and befriend them. They remove the ills which now beset you, and show you how to prevent future ills. The friendship of the wise and the noble is more precious than any material wealth. If you are in a position of authority, ensure that you are surrounded by such people, for they are your eyes and your mind. No enemy can defeat you, if you have wise and noble advisors – and if you take their advice.

Valluvar 421–427, 431–433, 441–446

Good company and careful thought

If you wish to be great, avoid the company of those whose minds are small and mean. Just as soil colours water, so companions colour the mind. The five senses are constantly filling the mind with perceptions; but companions determine how those perceptions are understood. Wisdom seems to come from within the mind; but in truth it comes from enjoying the company of the wise. Pure thoughts and pure actions come from pure company.

Before undertaking any action, assess its cost and its benefit – and then subtract the cost from the benefit, to determine its value. If you cannot make this calculation alone, take the advice of others. Nothing is impossible for those whose actions are preceded by careful thought and wise counsel. Do not risk your capital for the sake of high interest; do not embark on any new venture, without assessing the possibility of failure.

Before undertaking any action, weigh up your own strength, the strength of your allies, and the strength of your opponents. Nothing is impossible for those who ensure that they have sufficient support. Those who are guided by enthusiasm and zeal, rather than by rational calculation, will soon perish. Those who are too proud to adapt their plans in the face of superior opposition, will be quickly defeated.

Valluvar 451–455, 461–464, 471–474

The right means and the right time

A peacock's feather can break the axle of an over-loaded cart. A boy climbing too high up a tree, may step on a branch which breaks under his weight. Do what is within your capacity, and do not try to do more; give within your means, and do not try to give more. If your income is small, your expenditure should also be small – then you will think yourself rich. Those whose generosity exceeds their wealth, soon cease to be generous.

A crow can defeat an owl, if it attacks the owl by day; you can defeat your opponents, if you choose the right time to attack them. The rope which attaches you to good fortune, is made of shrewd timing. Nothing is impossible if you choose the right means, and deploy them at the right time. A king can conquer the world, if he is willing calmly to bide his time. To retreat in the face of superior force, is the prelude to victory.

Do not despise your opponents; and do not start a battle, until you can see how you will win it. A strong fortress in which to retreat and wait, is a great advantage even to men of valour. Even weak people can win their battles, if they choose the right place and time to defend and attack. A crocodile wins in water, but out of the water it is easily vanquished; an elephant can defeat men with spears, but in a bog jackals can overcome it.

Valluvar 475–478, 481–486, 491–495, 500

Energy and achievement

Anger is bad; but worse than anger is complacency. Complacency destroys a person's reputation, as lack of study destroys the intellect; complacency and honour can never combine. Just as cowardice never wins battles, so complacency never wins good fortune.

Compassion is the most gracious of virtues; it can move the world. Compassion is the mark of humanity; without compassion a person is a burden on the earth. What use is a song that cannot be sung; what use are eyes without sympathy? Like a tree rooted in the ground, a pitiless heart cannot be moved.

Your possessions may be stolen or sold, and then belong to someone else; but your vigour can never be taken by others. Vigour is a far greater asset than gold or land; to people of vigour the loss of wealth causes no anxiety, because new wealth will always find its way to them. The lotus rises as high as the water; people rise as high as their vigour. If you aim high, failure is as good as success.

The smoke of indolence dims the light of virtue. If you wish to improve yourself through life, you should keep indolence at bay. There are three marks of indolence: procrastination, forgetfulness, and excessive sleep.

> *Valluvar* 531–534, 571–573, 576, 591–596,
> 601–602, 605

Fortune and misfortune

When a task proves difficult, do not declare it to be impossible; try harder. The world despairs of those who despair; stick to the tasks which you have undertaken. There is no greater satisfaction than persisting in a difficult task, and finally accomplishing it. Failure caused by bad luck is never despised; but failure through lack of exertion is regarded with contempt.

If you laugh at misfortune, you will not be overcome by it. Misfortune may rise like a flood; but bold thoughts will quell it. If you refuse to be grieved by grief, then grief itself will grieve. If you refuse to be troubled by trouble – if you are like a bull pulling a cart through mud – then trouble will be troubled. Never complain during times of poverty, and never crow during times of prosperity. Those who do not despair at misfortune, remain serene at the advent of good fortune. Those who are not elated by good fortune, take misfortune in their stride.

Regard pain as pleasure, and misfortune as fortune; then your opponents will never defeat you.

Valluvar 611–613, 618, 621–626, 628–630

Advice and eloquence

When someone asks you for advice, show compassion and concern; make an effort to inform yourself thoroughly about the matters at hand; and then speak with firmness and clarity. Your advice should be aimed at bringing happiness to the person seeking it, and harmony to the neighbourhood in which the person lives. If you sharpen your intellect with constant study, your advice will frequently be sought. Yet, even if you have read widely and deeply, your advice should always be practical.

Eloquence is a rare gift; yet since speech is a powerful tool, the gift of eloquence should be closely guarded. Eloquent speakers charm those who hear them; and thus people seek out their company. Eloquence should be used to induce virtue; and it should never be used to convey lies and falsehoods. A good teacher combines eloquence with wisdom. But eloquence should not be combined with verbosity; those who are brief and concise, are more likely to avoid errors.

Do not do or say anything that you will later regret. When you have acted or spoken after careful thought, do not later regret what you have done or said. Do not do or say anything which the wise would condemn; it is better to be poor with a clear conscience, than to be rich with a guilty conscience. Those who deliberately speak or act wrongly, may get their way; but in the end they will come to grief.

Valluvar 632–633, 636–637, 641–646,
649–650, 655–658

Efficiency and deliberation

Efficiency consists in strength of mind. You should strive to avoid disaster and ruin; but if disaster and ruin confront you, do not weaken. Let your actions reveal your aims; do not reveal your intentions in advance. Talk is easy, but action is hard; but if your mind remains strong, you will accomplish your aims. You may be small, but that does not imply weakness; a linchpin holds a wheel in place. Decide with a clear mind what you intend to do – and, once you have reached your decision, act without delay.

The purpose of deliberation is decision; to deliberate and to dither is bad. When it is wise to delay, then delay; but when there is nothing to be gained by delay, then act. If your first course of action proves ineffective, then consider other courses. But do not start a course of action, and then stop half way through; this is as useless as trying to put out half a fire. Let one action lead to another, as one elephant can lead a hunter to another.

When you are opposed in your actions by an enemy, consider carefully how to react. First, make friends with the enemies of your enemy. If you are now stronger than your enemy, continue in your actions. But if you are too weak, then seek a compromise.

Valluvar 661–664, 666–668, 671–674, 678–680

Spiritual advancement through friendship

Those who know the thoughts of a friend, without the friend speaking, are like jewels in the earth. The ability to know the thoughts of friends is a sign of spiritual wisdom; through spiritual discipline people acquire this priceless capacity. Outwardly such people appear quite ordinary; but inwardly they are extraordinary. Their eyes can look at a friend's face, and read the mind that lies behind it.

True friends are like good books; they are a perpetual delight. The purpose of friendship is the acquisition of spiritual wisdom; friends support one another on the spiritual path. Friends know by intuition each other's feelings; when they smile at one another, their smiles come from their hearts. Ask your friends to correct you when you go wrong; and correct them when they go wrong. Ask your friends to share their sorrows and anxieties with you; and share your sorrows and anxieties with them. When you feel your clothes slipping, you swiftly reach out to hold them up; when friends are in need, go to their aid with equal speed.

Do not make friends rashly, because you can never abandon a friend; if you make friends in haste, you will repent at leisure. Seek friends with the wisdom and the courage to correct you when you go astray.

Valluvar 701–705, 783–788, 791–792, 795

Folly, conceit and malice

Folly consists in grasping what is bad, and letting slip what is good. The folly of follies is to love what is corrupt. Fools lack any sense of shame; they lack curiosity; they lack love for other living beings; and they lack respect for those wiser than themselves. There is no greater fool than someone who has studied many books, and yet lacks self-control. The harm that fools do to themselves, far exceeds any harm their enemies can do.

Conceit consists in pretending to be wise. When people pretend to have knowledge which they do not possess, their genuine knowledge is called into question. Can conceited people be regarded as clothed, when their pretences are exposed? Conceit condemns people to perpetual ignorance, because it convinces them that they have nothing to learn.

Malice consists in hating all life; but only a fool responds to malice with malice. People who cast out the hatred in their hearts, are treated as friends by everyone – and the space that malice once took, is filled with joy. Who wants to fight against a person free of malice? To fight against hatred is the path to glory; to yield to hatred is the path to disgrace.

Valluvar 831–834, 843–846, 848, 851–855, 858

Drinking, gambling, gluttony and miserliness

A lover of wine strikes no fear in his enemies; they mock him as his glory wanes. If you are indifferent to the judgement of the wise, then drink freely; but if you value their good opinion, abstain. The joviality of a drunken man disgusts even his own mother; she turns her face away from him. Drunkards suffer from the worst kind of ignorance: they are ignorant of themselves. Drunkards are dead, even while they are alive; wine is their poison.

To win at gambling is worse than to lose; it induces you to gamble again. Can a gambler ever thrive, when every win is followed by a hundred losses? Not only does gambling destroy wealth; it destroys hearts and minds as well.

Let your body fully digest one meal, before you eat another meal; then you will rarely need medicines. Eat sparingly; and only eat when you are hungry; then you will rarely suffer pain. As health attaches itself to a moderate eater, so disease sticks to a glutton. Those who eat without limit, have illnesses without limit.

To a miser wealth is as useless as a corpse. Misers who worship wealth, are haunted by it. By refusing to share or to spend what they possess, they live like paupers. If wealth is neither enjoyed nor given away, it is a curse. Wealth which is hoarded, is like a beautiful woman who never marries.

Valluvar 921–926, 931–932, 938, 942–947,
1001–1002, 1005–1007

Service, agriculture and poverty

There is nothing more glorious than to work for the good of your neighbours. A combination of zeal and wisdom can transform a village or town. Destiny itself girds its loins, and rushes to help those who help others – and ensures success to their endeavours. People will flock to anyone who is capable of leading them. So if you possess the gift of leadership, use it in the service of your community.

The hardest job in this world is farming; but it is also the best. Ploughmen are the earth's axle pin; they carry the whole world. There is nothing finer than eating food which you yourself have grown. Even the greatest emperor depends on ploughmen to produce the food which he and his soldiers need. Those who eat what their own hands produce, neither beg from others, nor turn away others begging from them.

There is nothing to compare with poverty; only poverty is like poverty. It is a tyrant which oppresses both the bodies and the hearts of its subjects. Those who are crushed by poverty, lose self-respect and gentleness; their faces grow dark with despair, and their speech becomes harsh. The misery of poverty attracts countless other miseries to itself.

Valluvar 1021–1026, 1031–1035, 1041–1045

Knowledge of God

In order to distinguish truth from falsehood – the eternal from that which is not eternal – it is necessary to renounce all interest in the fruit of your actions, both in this life and beyond. It is necessary to become inwardly tranquil, controlling the senses and the mind. Only in this state is it possible for you to perceive the eternal, which is God.

The complete knowledge of God is the highest end to which a human being can aspire. Knowledge of God destroys the root of all evil, which is ignorance. Hence you should nurture within yourself the desire to know God.

There may appear to be a puzzle regarding knowledge of God. If human beings already know God, why do they need to aspire to knowledge of him? But if they do not already know God, how can they know he exists?

The answer to this puzzle is that true knowledge is God. God is all the powers that comprise true knowledge: purity, intelligence and freedom. God is the true knowledge that already exists in every living being – which we call the soul. To be aware of our own existence is to be aware of the existence of the soul; and it is impossible to deny existence.

Sankara 1:1.1

The ultimate cause

God is the origin of the world; he sustains the world; and he will destroy the world. The world has many types of living being, each distinguished by its name and form. The world is the place where all living beings act, and where their actions have effects. Every action, and every effect of every action, has a place and a time. God is the ultimate cause of all living beings; and hence he is the ultimate cause of all actions.

The world could not have originated for any other entity except that entity which is true knowledge. And it could not have occurred spontaneously without a cause; since every effect has a cause, there must be an ultimate cause – which is God.

God is not an object of the senses; he has no connection with any kind of sensual perception. The senses have only external things as their objects; thus they cannot have God as an object. We perceive through the senses the effects of God, but not God himself.

Sankara 1:1.2

Divine salvation

God is eternal and omniscient; he is self-sufficient; he is perfectly pure, infinitely intelligent, and utterly free; he is total knowledge and absolute bliss. Those who meditate devoutly on God, attain salvation.

This salvation is infinite and eternal; it cannot undergo any changes; it is not composed of separate parts; it does not depend on any external light, but lights itself. Nothing can affect salvation; it is beyond good and evil, and beyond the process of cause and effect. Thus salvation is divine; through meditating on God, you become God – or, rather, you realize that the soul within you is God.

It is impossible to conceive of God as separate from the soul. Since God is omnipresent, he must be present within every living being – and this presence is what we mean by the soul. Moreover, it is impossible to conceive of salvation as something external to the soul, to be attained by external activities such as the performance of rituals. If salvation were attained by external activities, it would imply that these activities in some way created salvation – in which case it could not be divine.

Sankara 1:1.4

The soul knowing the soul

The soul cannot be different from that which knows the soul. Since the soul is eternal, that which knows the soul must also be eternal; a transient entity could not know an eternal entity. Thus we can conclude that knowledge of the soul consists in the soul knowing itself.

The soul cannot be different within one living being than within another. Since the soul is infinite, it has no bounds; it is uniform and limitless. Thus the soul is the soul of all living beings.

Hence the soul cannot be denied – the soul cannot deny itself. The soul cannot be affected by injunctions – the soul cannot change. The soul cannot be striven after, nor can it be avoided – the soul is there.

Perishable things perish because they are not the soul; they are merely external manifestations of the soul. The soul is imperishable, because nothing finite can make it perish – nothing finite and transient can affect that which it infinite and eternal.

Sankara 1:1.4

Knowing the soul

Those who attain true knowledge of the soul, are free from the body, even while they are alive. Those who understand that God and the soul are one, are no longer bound to the cycle of birth, death and rebirth. But those who do not understand that the soul and God are one, remain bound to the cycle.

Consider an empty jar. People might talk about 'the space inside the jar'; and this expression seems to suggest that the space inside the jar is separate from other space. In the same way a person may talk about 'my soul'; and this expression seems to suggest that the soul within an individual is separate from the soul within other individuals – and hence separate from God. In truth the space within an empty jar is the same as space elsewhere; there is simply space. And the soul within one individual is the same as the soul within another; there is simply soul – which is God.

Sankara 1:1.4–5

Devotion and knowledge

God is conceived under two forms. First he is conceived within the limiting conditions of a body; and secondly he is conceived as free from all limiting conditions.

Sometimes it seems that God has a double nature. Those who conceive him within the limiting conditions of a body, make him the object of devotion. And since different groups of people conceive him in different bodies, there are many different modes of devotion. Some groups conceive God within a body of great beauty; so their devotion is marked by praise. Some groups conceive God within a body who works hard in the service of others; so their devotion is marked by also working hard in the service of others. But in all these different modes of devotion, the soul within the body is the true object of devotion; and since the soul is divine, each mode is valid.

Those who conceive of God as free from all limiting conditions, seek to know him in the fullness of his power and glory. Yet they do not attain this knowledge immediately. Rather their conception of God rises through a graduated series of beings, each more powerful and glorious than the last.

Sankara I:I.II

The universal soul and the embodied soul

We distinguish between the universal soul which is free from the body, and knows itself; and the embodied soul, which acts in the world, enjoys the pleasures of the senses, and is bound by ignorance.

The distinction may be compared to that between a juggler and a magician. The juggler stands on solid ground, and throws objects in the air; everyone can see what he is doing. The magician operates by creating illusions – such as the rope trick in which he appears to be climbing a rope towards the sky. The juggler is admired because people know what he is doing; the magician is admired because people are ignorant of what he is doing. Yet the skill of the juggler and the skill of the magician are much the same.

The distinction may also be compared with that between the atmosphere all around us, and the atmosphere within a closed jar. The atmosphere all around us is free, whereas the atmosphere in the jar is trapped. Yet in truth there is only one atmosphere.

Sankara 1:1.17

Growing in knowledge and bliss

As you grow in knowledge, you see the soul within the body attaining unity with the universal soul, which is God. Actually the embodied soul and the universal soul are eternally united; as you grow in knowledge, you become more and more aware of this unity. The universal soul consists of bliss; so awareness of unity brings awareness of bliss. And once awareness of unity is complete, the soul within your body breaks free from the constraints of the body; you break free from the bonds of birth, death and rebirth.

But while you make even the smallest distinction between the soul within your body and the universal soul, you remain bound within the body – and hence bound on the wheel of birth, death and rebirth. And while you remain bound within the body, your experience of bliss is partial, and you continue to experience pain and fear. Complete absence of pain, and complete spiritual bliss, only comes with complete awareness of unity between the embodied soul and the universal soul.

Sankara 1:1.19

The effects of the embodied soul

The embodied soul makes choices and takes decisions; and on the basis of these choices and decisions, it undertakes courses of action. If these actions are good, the embodied soul acquires merit; if these actions are bad, the embodied soul loses merit. The actions may cause pleasure to the embodied soul, and to the soul within other bodies; or they may cause pain to the embodied soul, and to the soul within other bodies. Thus the embodied soul has many effects.

The universal soul does not make choices, nor take decisions; and it does not act. Thus it cannot acquire merit or lose merit; and it cannot cause pleasure or pain. In short, the universal soul has no effects.

Moreover the effects of the embodied soul do not impinge on the universal soul.

Sankara 1:2.8

From ignorance to knowledge

The embodied soul is bound and constrained by ignorance. In the twilight of evening you may see a figure, and assume it is a man; but in fact it is a post. In the same way in a state of ignorance you assume that the soul within your heart belongs to you; you identify yourself with the soul. But in fact the soul within your heart is the universal soul. In your ignorance you say: 'I am my soul.' You should say: 'The soul within me is God.'

How, then, can you replace ignorance with knowledge? You must discard the information which the senses constantly pass to the mind; this information consists of many small parts, which appear separate and unconnected. As you discard this information, you will become aware of the unity of all things; and you will realize that the source of this unity is the soul, which is present in all living beings and all objects. In short, you must stop discriminating, and start unifying.

Sankara 1:3.19

The cause of all causes

We may distinguish between two types of cause: the material cause and the operative cause. The effect of a material cause is in essence the same as the cause itself; whereas the effect of an operative cause is quite distinct from the cause. Consider a potter using a lump of clay to make a pot. The lump of clay is the material cause of the pot, and in essence is the same as the pot. The potter is the operative cause, and is manifestly quite distinct from the pot.

What is the ultimate cause of all material causes? Since God is the origin of all material things, he must be the ultimate material cause. What is the ultimate operative cause of all operative causes? Since God is the guiding principle of all that happens, God must be the ultimate operative cause. Thus in truth material causes and operative causes are one. If this were not so, it would follow that everything could not be known through one thing.

Since the soul is God's presence in the world, we may say that the soul is the ultimate cause of all material and operative causes.

Sankara 1:4.23

The illusion of different states

A magician is not at any time affected by the magical effects which he produces, because he knows they are unreal. In the same way the soul is not affected by the effects which it produces in the world.

Human beings are not affected by the visions which are witnessed in dreams, because these visions do not continue in the waking state, or in the state of dreamless sleep. The soul witnesses every dream, witnesses every event that occurs in the waking state, and also witnesses the dreaming state; but it is not touched by any of these states. Just as the magician knows that his magical effects are illusions, so the soul knows that all three human states are illusions.

It is quite common at twilight for a person to see a piece of rope lying on the ground, and imagine it to be a snake. To the soul dreams, waking events, and dreamless sleep are as insubstantial as that snake.

Sankara 2:1.9

The authority of sacred texts

We should treat the sacred texts, which have been passed down to us from ancient times, with the greatest respect. Even if our reason is confused by these texts, or is inclined to refute them, nonetheless we should rely on the teachings of these texts.

Human thoughts are unfettered, with nothing to constrain them; thus human reasoning lacks any stability. A clever man, whose capacity for rational thought has been great, may argue that the sacred texts are mistaken in certain respects. Then another man, who is even cleverer, may show that the first man's arguments are fallacious; and this second man may argue that the sacred texts are mistaken in other respects. Then another man, who is cleverer still, may show that the second man's arguments are fallacious; and this third man may argue that the sacred texts are mistaken in other respects. And so on. The sheer diversity of people's opinions shows that reason is not reliable.

We cannot overcome this difficulty by declaring that some particular person possesses supreme mental powers, and that we shall rely on this person's opinions as authoritative. In due course we shall find someone of equal mental powers, who holds contrary opinions.

True knowledge, on which spiritual salvation depends, cannot be attained by rational thought alone. It can only be attained with the guidance of the sacred texts.

Sankara 2:1.11

Creation as God's sport

Consider a prince whose every desire has been satisfied; he has no unfulfilled wishes. Yet he does not become inactive. On the contrary, he engages in all manner of activities in order to amuse himself. His activities have no purpose beyond themselves; they are sport.

Consider the process of breathing in and breathing out. We do not make a decision to breathe in and out; we do not conceive some purpose for this activity. Breathing follows from our nature as human beings, regardless of any deliberate intention.

The activities of God may be compared both to those of the prince and to breathing. God has no purpose in creating the world beyond the act itself; the existence of the world is not the means to some further end. And the nature of the world proceeds from God's own nature.

To our limited minds the creation of the world seems a vastly complex and hazardous undertaking; but to God it is no more than a game. And if in ordinary life we may detect, by close scrutiny, some subtle ulterior motives in the games which people play, we can find no ulterior motive in the actions of God.

But in considering creation, we should remember that it does not belong to the highest order of reality; it belongs to the sphere of appearances, which reflect God, but are not in themselves divine.

Sankara 2:1.33

Actions and their consequences

Should we blame God for the inequalities in the world? Is God responsible for some people being rich, and some poor; is he responsible for some people enjoying good health, and some suffering persistent disease? Should we blame God for the cruelty in the world? Is God responsible for tyrannical rulers oppressing their subjects, and for stronger animals eating weaker animals?

In creating the world God bound himself by the moral law. This law states that some actions are good, and have good consequences; while other actions are bad, and have bad consequences. Thus individual beings are able to make choices; and the inequalities and cruelties in this world are the consequences of bad choices.

Kind and gentle actions are good, and lead to equality. Cruel and harsh actions are bad, and lead to inequality. We are each responsible for our own actions, and for the consequences of our actions.

Sankara 2:1.34

The eternity of creation

The notion that the world had no beginning, commends it-self to reason. If the world had a beginning, it would follow that, as it sprang into existence, the soul voluntarily gave up its freedom, and entered hundreds of millions of bodies – thereby binding itself to the cycle of birth, death, and rebirth. This is inconceivable.

It would also follow that the initial distribution of good and evil occurred arbitrarily, without reference to previous good and bad actions. Yet, as we have seen, God cannot be held responsible for the inequality of good and bad, pleasure and pain, in the world. We may say that ignorance is the cause of inequality, in that people act badly because they are ignorant of how to control their anger, hatred and other passions.

We can conclude that there was no moment of creation, at which God brought the world into existence. Bodies have existed for all eternity; the soul has dwelt in bodies for all eternity; and there has been good and bad for all eternity. Creation is eternal.

Sankara 2:1.36

Failure to distinguish body and soul

God and the embodied soul stand in relation to each other as the one acting, and the one being acted upon. The embodied soul is part of God, just as a spark is part of the fire. By 'part' we do not mean a distinct entity, because God is not composed of parts in this sense. We mean that, just as the spark is of the essence of the fire, so the embodied soul is of the essence of God.

The pain which an embodied soul feels from time to time, is not real, but imaginary. It is caused by ignorance, by which there is a failure to distinguish between the soul and the body. In a state of ignorance people imagine that pain felt by the body is also affecting the soul. This ignorance is common to all living beings; and it finds expression in such phrases as, 'I come', 'I go', 'I am blind', 'I am confused' and so on. In these phrases the 'I' refers to the soul; yet the soul cannot come or go, be blind or confused and so on.

The only way of dispelling this ignorance is through perfect knowledge; without perfect knowledge the ignorance will remain.

Sankara 2:3.43, 46, 48

Forms of the soul

Light from the sun or the moon passes through space, and
then comes into contact with the earth. As it does so, it takes
the shape of the earth and the objects on the earth; it becomes
bent, curved and straight according to the shape of each object. In the same way the soul assumes the shape of the living beings which it enters.

For this reason in their meditations and devotions human
beings can envisage the soul – and hence God – in any shape
or form that they wish. It is wrong to teach that the soul has
no form, and therefore cannot be envisaged. Equally it is
wrong to teach that the soul has a particular form, and should
only be envisaged in that form. The soul has any and every
form.

Sankara 3:2.15

The permanence of consciousness

Some people say that consciousness consists in the perceptions which come from the senses, and the thoughts which arise from those perceptions. Yet there is a contradiction in this view. If it were true, it would imply that perceptions of the senses are both the objects of consciousness and consciousness itself – which is absurd. Thus we must acknowledge that consciousness is separate and distinct from external perceptions.

Indeed, consciousness is the essence of the soul. And since the soul is distinct from the body and its senses, therefore consciousness must be separate and distinct from the perceptions of the senses.

Since the soul is permanent and eternal, it follows that consciousness is permanent. This permanence finds expression in such phrases as, 'I recall seeing this', and 'I remember hearing that'. In these phrases the objects of memory are transient things which the senses have perceived; but the subject is permanent. If the subject were not permanent, it would be impossible to recall or remember a perception after the perception had occurred.

Sankara 3:3.54

The consequence of knowledge

The consequence of knowledge is the release of the soul from the constraints of the body – and hence from the cycle of birth, death and rebirth. Release is not achieved or brought about, because it is the natural and permanent state of the soul. Rather it is realized through knowledge.

It follows that we cannot distinguish higher and lower knowledge; knowledge, by its very nature, is high. Knowledge differs from one person to another only in the speed of attainment; one person may attain knowledge quickly, and another may attain it slowly. But the release of the soul, which is the consequence of knowledge, cannot differ. Moreover, the consequence of lack of knowledge, which is the bondage of the soul, is the same in all cases.

Yet knowledge may be partial. By this we mean that people may know some of God's qualities, but not all of them. It may be tempting, therefore, to speak of inequalities between people – to say that one person is superior to another person, because the former has greater knowledge. But this would be misleading. When perfect knowledge is attained, the qualities of God are discerned as a single, infinite quality – or, more precisely, God is discerned as devoid of qualities.

Sankara 3:4.52

THE YOGA OF DEVOTION

In south India in the seventh century there was a strong re-
action against the austere, philosophical religion of the Jains,
who were dominant, in favour of an emotional form of piety,
in which poetry and music were central. The finest hymns
were written by a wandering sage known as Apparswami.

In north India three centuries later Muslim invasions destroyed the educational system which had produced philoso-
phers; and popular poets and musicians took their place. One
of the earliest of these was Devara Dasimayya, who had a
vision telling him to love God and other people with his heart.

Two centuries later Basavanna (d. 1168), from a wealthy
high-caste household, attracted a large community of disciples,
to whom he taught both the yoga of devotion and the rejection of caste. Little is known of Lal Ded, the first of the two
great women poets, except that she lived in Kashmir, probably
early in the fourteenth century. Allama Prabhu, many of whose
poems are strange allegories, spent much of his life in a trance,
and was regarded by his contemporaries as mad. Mirabai
(d.c. 1400), the second great female poet, was a princess, who
left her palace and wandered from temple to temple.

Ravidas was a leather worker, making him an outcast in
Hindu society; a strong vein of social protest runs through his
devotional verses. Tulsidas (d. 1623) was born into a family
of beggars, and experienced religion as an escape from the
humiliation of his childhood; his central theme is the power
of God's name. Ramprasad (d.1795), a clerk in an office in Calcutta, wrote verses on office paper, addressing God as Mother.

A vision of God

My God is truth; and in truth he has proclaimed me as his own.

I see my God. I see the moon in his tangled hair. I see a garland of flowers around his neck. I see an earring made of pearl in each ear. I see him wearing a cloak made from the hide of an elephant. When his cloak blows in the wind, I see beneath it his naked body, smooth and shining. I see a glittering crown on his head. I see ash smeared on his face. Nothing can defile my God.

Yes, God is here at his shrine. When did he choose to build his shrine in this place? Was it at the time when he burned up death? Was it at that time when he turned the flame of lust onto itself? Was it at the moment of creation, when he called the earth and the sky into being?

Apparswami 26, 27, 28

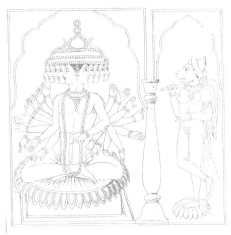

Stained with sin

I have no right to live, because day by day I have stained my-self with sin. Lord, I have read your sacred texts; but my stubborn mind has refused to understand their meaning or follow their guidance. I have not allowed your fire to burn in my heart. When I have seen your footprints on the ground – footprints shaped like the lotus flower – I have walked in the opposite direction.

I have sunk deeper and deeper in the mire of wickedness. I have sought knowledge of which I should have remained ignorant; and I have ignored knowledge which I should have sought. I have treated vice as if it were my dearest friend. Save me, Lord; reach out to me with your grace. I do not ask to see your face; a glimpse of your feet would give me hope.

I am like a fickle lover. I have always loved you, Lord, but I have never been faithful. When I should have clung firmly to you, I have chased after other sources of pleasure. I have swung towards you and away from you like a pendulum. Let me lie at your feet – and never stir.

Apparswami 29, 30, 31

The sea of life

Violence rages in my heart; my body is like a cage in which
a restless tiger prowls. In my anguish I have broken the divine spoon – the spoon with which I used to consume God's
grace. I feel as if I am a frog in the mouth of a snake: I am
gripped by terror, but cannot escape. Lord, look upon me
with love, and save me.

I am tossed about on the surging sea of life. My heart is
no more than a flimsy raft, and my mind is merely a pole;
the raft gives no protection against the rocks of desire, and
the pole cannot steer me through the currents of confusion.
Lord, replace my folly with your wisdom, and save me.

I am not a wild beast, and yet I behave like one. Will I
never know your peace, O God? Must I beg in vain? For what
purpose was I born into this world?

Apparswami 33, 34, 35

God's revelation

God, you have fixed my thoughtless mind, so that I think only of you. You have taught me that which human beings cannot teach themselves. You have shown me that which human eyes cannot see. You have told me that which no human tongue can express. You have pursued me, and made me your own. You have healed the diseases of my heart, and made me pure. Yes, you have revealed yourself to me.

Lord, you are my mother and my father. You are all the relatives I need. To me you are more beautiful than the most beautiful woman. You are all the riches that I could ever want. You are my family, my friends and my home. I leave behind all of the goods of this world; I abandon the deceitful glitter of gold and jewels. You alone are my wealth.

No one human being can hold sway over me. Death holds no fears for me. Nothing can grieve my heart or disturb my mind. Pain and sorrow cannot trouble me. Day by day I am filled with joy; and year by year that joy never diminishes. Lord, I am yours, and your bliss is mine. You are my king; you alone reign over me.

Apparswami 36, 38, 40

Balancing the world

Lord, you balance the world on your fingers, as a dancer balances a pot on her head. You keep the sky above the earth without any columns or pillars. What other gods could do this?

When a child is in the mother's womb, the child cannot see the mother's face, and the mother cannot see the child's face. When we are in the world, we cannot see the face of God; and we shield our own faces from the gaze of God.

Why does my body not obey my will? Why does your body not obey your will? I conclude that my body does not truly belong to me, and that your body does not truly belong to you. The body is a poor companion to the soul.

The snake of hatred bites the flesh, and its venom spreads through the body, from the soles of the feet to the top of the head. Only God can overcome the snake, and suck out the poison.

There is fire when people speak and act in righteous anger. There is fire when a man loves his wife, and a woman loves her husband. There is fire when men want food after labouring in the fields. There is fire when people are oppressed and exploited. God kindles these fires.

Devara Dasimayya 4, 23, 24, 25, 26

Grain in a tattered sack

A man puts grain in a tattered sack. He walks all night to the market, constantly afraid of being attacked by wild animals or robbed by thieves. He does not notice that the grain is falling out through the tatters. When he arrives at the market, the sack is empty. That is an image of the devotion of those with faint hearts.

Only wealthy men are able to be generous. Only strong men are able to be heroes. Most of us can only offer small gifts to those in need, and perform only modest acts of courage. Not every flower bears fruit.

For what purpose should I wield a sword, O Lord? Who should I pierce with my sword, and to whom should I show mercy? All the world and its inhabitants belong to you.

Is the universe your body, O Lord? Are the elements the flesh of your body? Are the sun and the moon organs of your body? When I look at the beauty of the universe, I see you. If I were to harm any part of the universe, I should be injuring you.

Devara Dasimayya 42, 43, 44, 45

Devotion to devotees

For your devotees, O Lord, I shall be a bullock, pulling the cart on which they ride. I shall be a servant, cleaning the houses in which they live. I shall be a watchdog, guarding the land which they own. To those who raise their arms in devotion to you, I shall be devoted. I shall even be the hedge of thorns around their gardens.

There is a chain of eighteen links which binds us to the world. Its links are past, present, and future acts; the body and the mind; wealth and furniture; the instinct for survival, and the desire for respect; gold and land; spouse; lust and anger; greed and infatuation; pride and envy. Each of us is like a dog on a leash.

The earth is a gift from you to us. Growing crops are a gift from you to us. The gentle breeze is a gift from you to us. How should I treat those men and women who never praise you? They are no better than dogs and bitches eating out of your hand.

Whoever it was that built this earth, set it on a firm foundation, filled it with all kinds of living things, set the wind in motion and the moon on its course, covered it with the sky, and finally put himself within it. That is the one to whom I pray.

Devara Dasimayya 49, 72, 80, 87

A fox standing in wonder

He will make sinners roam the streets as homeless beggars. He will use them as pestles for grinding grain. He will slash them, as if they were sticks of sugar cane, in order to look inside. If they do not cry with pain and tremble with fear, he will pick them up in his hands and shake them. Yes, our God will do all that.

Can a fox ever stand in wonder at the glory of God? Can a fox ever meditate on the beauty of God? Can he wander the globe as a pilgrim? Can he bathe in a thousand sacred rivers? Yes, all living beings can devote themselves to him. And for those who refuse, their activities are no more than idle games.

For those who are unified with God, there is no dawn, no new moon, no noonday, no equinoxes, no sunsets, and no full moons. Their homes are like the most sacred of cities.

I have a body, Lord, and you are its breath. You know the secret of my body, and I know the secret of your breath. You know, and I know, the miracle of your breath in my body.

I shall not put my feet where you have not trodden before; I shall follow your footsteps precisely, O Lord. Those who do not love you, cannot understand how my feet have become yours.

Devara Dasimayya 90, 94, 98, 120, 121

A body for God

Since I have a body, I feel hunger. Since I have a body, I must lie down and rest. Lord, do not taunt me for having a body. Take on a body yourself, and see how you feel.

A traveller in a desert prays for water, but finds none. A person in the depths of despair cries out for a word of comfort, but hears only an echo of the cry. Why do you not answer their requests?

Unless walls are erected, space cannot fill a house. Unless the eye sees, the mind cannot envisage forms. Unless a path is laid, human beings cannot reach God. How do we know that a path exists?

Fire can burn, but it cannot move. Wind can move, but it cannot burn. But if fire and wind combine, they can both burn and move. In this respect fire is like knowledge, and wind is like action.

Devara Dasimayya 123, 124, 126, 127

Male and female

When the trees are in bud, the wind carries nothing; but
when the buds open into flowers, the wind carries their fragrance far and wide. When a baby girl is born, her father and
mother know nothing of her future appearance; but when
childhood opens into adulthood, they can boast of her ample
breasts and flowing hair. Let us be patient in awaiting the full
consequences of God's actions.

God hovers over all he has made. Yet who can know his
beauty? He created all the forms and colours on earth. Yet
who can know his form and colour?

When people see someone with breasts and long hair,
they assume that person is a woman. When people see someone with a beard and whiskers, they assume that person is a
man. But what do people assume about the soul which dwells
in all human beings? The soul is neither male nor female.

Suppose you cut a stick of bamboo in two. You call the
bottom half a woman, and the top half a man. Then you rub
the two together, and kindle a fire. Is that fire male or female?

Devara Dasimayya 128, 131, 133, 144

Cries for help

The world is like a flood. It is rising up my body to my heart. It is rising up my breast to my throat. It is rising up my neck, and will soon cover my head. Lord, Lord, listen to my cries for help.

At the beginning of the month the light of the moon increases night by night; at the end of the month the light of the moon decreases night by night. My light has decreased night by night for so long, that now it has disappeared completely. When will you release me, O Lord, from this darkness?

When I dwelt in my mother's womb, I did not appreciate the ease and comfort of my situation. When I emerged from the womb, I soon learnt how hard this world is. Was it wrong to be born, O Lord? Have mercy on me for being born. I promise you that I shall never be born again.

A monkey leaps from branch to branch. My heart leaps from one passion to another. How can I trust my heart? How can I believe what my heart tells me? May my heart cling to only one passion – the passion for God.

Hounds chase a hare; lusts chase my body. The lusts catch my body. I cry out: 'Let go! Let go!' Lord, save me from these hounds, before they tear me apart.

Basavanna 8, 9, 21, 33, 36

A cow in a quagmire

I am like a cow who has fallen into a quagmire. The cow moos in this direction and that; but no one hears her, and no one goes out in search of her. Then God sees her, and lifts her out by the horns.

Cripple me, Lord; then I shall not do anything that will corrupt me. Blind me, Lord; then I shall not see anything that will corrupt me. Deafen me, Lord; then I shall not hear anything that will corrupt me. Keep me close beside you.

To whom do I belong? I ask that question daily. To whom does that person belong? Others ask that question about me. Let this be the answer: that I belong to God.

Lord, you have no mercy; Lord, you have no heart. Why did you bring me to birth in this wretched, miserable world? I beg you to make something that belongs to me alone, and will bring me comfort. A little tree, or even a plant, would suffice.

A mother watches over her children, guiding their actions; she tells them not to put their hands in a fire, or to walk in the path of a cobra. Lord, watch over me, guiding my actions; keep me from every danger – physical and spiritual.

Basavanna 52, 59, 62, 64, 70

A rock in water

When I arrive at a house, and see weeds around the door and dirt within, I conclude that the owner of the house is absent. When I consider myself, and see the deceit and lust that corrupts my heart, I conclude that God is absent.

It makes no difference how long a rock soaks in water; the rock remains hard. It does not matter how long I spend in worship; my heart remains hard. My efforts to please God are futile.

If a prostitute with a baby has a client, neither the baby nor the client has enough of her. When she goes to comfort the baby, the client shouts; when she is with the client, the baby cries. If I try to serve both God and money, I fail God and remain poor.

A woman goes off to fornicate, but derives no pleasure. She sits down to rest against an old wall, but scorpions sting her. She goes home in shame, and her husband thrashes her. She wishes she had stayed at home. That is an image of my life.

Basavanna 97, 99, 101, 111

Tongs joining hands

See-saw watermills bow their heads. But does that mean they are worshipping God? Tongs join hands. But does that mean they are praying to God? Parrots repeat words. But does that mean they are praising God? Lord, how do you want people to worship you, pray to you, and praise you?

A lamb is brought to a festival, in order to be killed and eaten; and flowers are brought to the festival, to be used as decorations. The lamb munches the flowers and consumes them. It knows nothing of the festival, and only wishes to fill its belly. So is it innocent of theft? But those who then kill the lamb, know what they are doing. Are they guilty of murder?

If people are injured, they ask their friends to tend them. If people lose their crops in a fire, they ask their friends for food. But if people acquire wealth, they forget their friends. Only when poverty strikes again, do they remember them.

The crookedness of the snake is straight enough for the snake-hole. The crookedness of the river is straight enough for the sea. But is the crookedness of priests straight enough for God?

Basavanna 125, 129, 132, 144

Preparing for old age

Before your hair turns grey, and wrinkles line your face; before your muscles wither, and your skin becomes a bag of bones; before your teeth fall out, and your back bends double; before you need a stick in order to walk; before the finger of death reaches out and touches you – worship the Lord.

Your body is now as strong as iron, and you can do whatever you want. But do not rely on your body's strength. Worship God, and prepare for the time when your body sags.

You are thrown into a river; a stone is tied to your foot, and a log is tied to your neck; the stone will not let you float, and the log will not let you sink. This is an image of the life which most people live: their sin prevents them from floating to God; but their righteousness prevents them from sinking into oblivion.

The root is the mouth of the tree; if you pour water at the bottom of the tree, green leaves sprout at the top. The mouth of the world is every man and woman; if they are nourished with truth, then the whole world flourishes.

Basavanna 161, 162, 350, 420

The numerous faces of God

Lord, you have eighty-four hundred thousand faces. Come, and show just one of your faces to me. If you do not show me one of your faces, I shall cease to dedicate myself to you, and commit myself to a human master instead. Lord, put on any of your faces, and reveal yourself to me.

I wash the holy statues, and then drink the water I have used. I eat the food that has been given by worshippers. Everything I consume, belongs to you, O Lord; everything I possess, belongs to you; my life and my honour is yours. You are like a prostitute, who insists on taking every last coin of her night's wages. Words are not enough for you; you demand everything.

My feet dance for you, and my tongue sings for you, Lord; and I cannot find peace. What else must I do, for you to pacify me? I worship you with my hands, but my heart is not at peace. What else must I do? I listen to the words of spiritual teachers, but they do not satisfy me. I should be willing to cut open my belly, if you would enter me and give me peace.

Basavanna 430, 468, 487

Singing with the heart

I cannot play any musical instruments; I refuse to beat the drums because I lack a sense of rhythm; and if I try to recite verse, I miss the metre of the lines. But, Lord, I sing to you with my heart.

Make my body the beam of a lute. Make my head the top of a drum. And make my nerves the strings of a lute. Hold me, Lord, and play me.

There are certain people who pretend to be holy. They stand at the doors of temples as the people enter. They offer to bless those who give them money, and to curse those who do not. Yet what power does a blessing or a curse possess, if it does not come from God?

The pot which holds our water is divine. The fan with which we separate the wheat from the chaff is divine. The stone flags which cover the floor of our house are divine. The strings of our lute are divine. The cups from which we drink, are divine. Whatever we touch with our hands, and wherever we place our feet, is divine. But there is only one God.

Fish love rivers that are full, and birds love trees that are in leaf. But you, Lord, also love rivers that have run dry, and trees that have withered. Do the fish and the birds understand this?

Basavanna 494, 500, 555, 563, 581

A fire burning

A priest has a sacred fire burning in his house. He treats the fire as if it were divine; and he constantly feeds it with wood, believing that this will win him divine blessing. One day he feeds it so much wood that the fire spreads, and his house starts to burn. He takes water from the drain to douse the flames, and dust from the street to smother them. The fire continues to burn, so he calls others to help him. Eventually they control the fire. The priest is extremely angry, and scolds the fire. How absurd! If the fire is divine, how can it do wrong? And if it is not divine, he should not have had it in his house.

A man went riding elephants. He dressed himself like a king. He did not take the truth with him; he had no intention of doing good. His elephant was pride, and his dress was arrogance. Soon the elephant threw him to the ground, and his dress was covered with mud.

Think of yourself as a stone. God will grind you until you are small; he will file you until your true nature shows. If your colour is bright, and the light shines through you, he will love you and cherish you – for you are a precious gem. But if your colour is dull, and no light can enter you, he will cast you aside.

Basavanna 586, 639, 686

A man and a woman for God

Sometimes I wear men's clothes, and I fight God's cause. Sometimes I wear women's clothes, and I care for God's people. I am a man for God, and I am a woman for God.

If the son of a poor man grows up to be a successful merchant, the poor man enjoys his son's riches. If the son of a weakling grows up to be a warrior, the coward boasts of his son's bravery. Make me rich, Lord, that my poor father may find comfort in his final years. Make me brave, Lord, that my weak father may hold his head high.

The rich make temples for God. But I am poor. Let my legs be the pillars, my body the shrine, and my head the dome.

I have only enough to feed my family, so I have nothing to give away. But I am not poor enough to beg, so I do not give others the opportunity to be generous. Am I useless?

Like a hailstone in warm sunlight, like wax close to a fire, I am melting with joy. The river of joy has broken its banks, and is pouring from my eyes. I have touched my Lord, and have joined myself to him.

                              Basavanna 703, 705, 820, 831, 847

A bowl and a mirror

Does your tongue have to express every religious thought which passes through your mind? Is it necessary to find verses from sacred texts to justify everything you do? Must you show off the marks which the Lord has made on your body?

Consider a bowl and a mirror: both are made of brass; one holds things, the other reflects things back. God wants you to be both a bowl and a mirror: he wants you to hold the love he has poured upon you; and he wants you to reflect his glory in your words and actions.

Calves do not consume all the milk which cows produce; fish do not need all the water which rivers produce; bees do not eat all the honey which flowers produce. Remember that you depend on things which other living beings have left over. So do not despise any living being; remember that all are created by God.

Basavanna 848, 860, 885

Mother's milk

Put your thoughts on the firm path that leads to immortality. If you allow them to stray from that path, they will fall into the soft mire of evil. As you walk along the path, do not be anxious or fearful, but be brave and determined.

The mind is like a baby; God is like the mother's breast; and the truth is like the milk that flows from the mother's breast. If the baby is restless, tossing from side to side, it will drink nothing, and it will eventually die; but if the baby remains quietly at the mother's breast, and sucks with all its strength, it will thrive.

There are men and women who see no distinction between themselves and all the other living beings who inhabit the earth. There are men and women who see no distinction between the day of joy and the night of sorrow. There are men and women whose minds are free from all duality. These men and women, and they alone, have seen the Lord, and know that he is the Lord of lords.

Lal Ded 12, 16

God as a beggar

For a moment I saw a river flowing. But I looked more closely, and could see no bridge by which to cross the river. So I realized that my vision was useless, and I felt sad.

For a moment I saw a bush. But I looked more closely, and saw that the bush had no buds, no flowers, and no fruits. So I realized that my vision was useless, and I felt sad.

For a moment I saw a cooking hearth blazing warmly. But I looked more closely, and saw no food to cook. So I realized that my vision was useless, and I felt sad.

For a moment I saw God disguised as a beggar. I looked more closely, and saw a potter's wife welcoming him into her home. I was the aunt of the potter's wife, and I also welcomed the beggar. I realized that I had seen the truth, and I was overjoyed.

Lal Ded 20

Asleep and awake

Some people, although they are sound asleep, are awake; other people, although they are awake, are asleep. Some people, although they bathe in sacred pools, are unclean; other people, although they are too busy to perform any religious rituals, are clean.

When you are born, God gives you a bag of coins. If you travel through life by the low road, you will spend those coins on selfish pleasures; so when you arrive at the river of death, you will have nothing left with which to pay for the ferry. If you travel through life by the high road, you will spend those coins on helping others; and when you arrive at the river, your bag will be fuller than at the beginning.

Think of the world as an ocean, and your life as a boat in which you are floating. Do you pray to God to steer your boat to the other side? Is he answering your prayer?

Lal Ded 22, 23, 25

Hurrying and relaxing

Hurry! Make haste! Rise up from your bed and run. The dawn is breaking, and you must rush to meet your divine friend. There is no time to lose. No; stop for a moment. Make yourself wings, and tie them to your feet. Then you can fly to meet your divine friend.

Relax! Slow down! Do not be anxious and afraid. Your divine friend, who was never born and will never die, is aware of you, and knows you are coming to him. Sit down, and eat the food which he provides for your journey. Pray to him for the strength you need.

God alone can save you. God alone can bring you to himself.

Lal Ded 27, 28

At the Lord's door

I wearied myself seeking my Lord. I exhausted myself searching for him in this place and that. I laboured for him beyond
my strength. I strove for him beyond my endurance. Finally
I arrived at his door, and found that bolts were pulled across.
I gazed at the door with eyes of love. The bolts slipped back,
and my Lord revealed himself to me.

Lal Ded 39

Water in a basket

Status and reputation are like water carried in a basket. Those who pride themselves on their strength, cannot catch the wind in their arms. Those who are admired for their skill, cannot tether an elephant with human hair.

If you carry water in a basket, I shall treat you with honour. If you clasp the wind to your bosom, I shall treat you as a hero. If you stop an elephant in its tracks with a hair of your head, I shall treat you as a king. Otherwise I shall treat you as I treat everyone else – as my equal under God.

Lal Ded 59

The wagon and the bee

Think of your body as a wagon, and your legs as its wheels.
The wagon is carrying all manner of precious goods to God.
The five senses are the drivers of the wagon, and they frequently disagree. Unless you control the drivers, ensuring that
they act correctly, the wagon will come off the road, and the
axle will break.

At springtime the cuckoo perches on the mango tree; and
the bird and the tree become one. Gooseberries are brought
from the mountains, and salt is brought from the sea, to
make pickle; in the cooking-pot the gooseberries and the salt
become one. I long to be one with my Lord.

Think of ignorance as a bee, the heart as a lotus, the soul
as a swan, and the body as the swan's cage. The bee is born
in the lotus, and flies upwards to the sky. It catches the wind
in its wings, and directs the wind to turn the world upside
down. But when the swan's cage is broken, the wings of the
bee break, and the bee falls to the ground.

Allama Prabhu 42, 59, 95

Camphor, mountains and a monkey

Think of knowledge as camphor, salvation as pearls, the universe as diamonds, and illusion sapphires. I saw my heart conceive the Lord, and I saw my hands and legs act according to his command. My nose smelled camphor, my eyes were dazzled by the gleam of pearls, and my mouth devoured diamonds. And in sapphires I could perceive countless people trying to hide.

Think of God's followers as mountains. If mountains shiver in the cold, in what can they be wrapped to keep them warm?

Think of the body as a city, life as the city gate, the mind as a monkey, the soul as a king, self-love as a wild elephant, the five senses as a snake with five hoods, and the lion as knowledge. I saw a monkey standing at the gate of a city. It mocked everyone that entered the city, even the king; before anyone had time to speak to the monkey, it started to utter abuse. I saw the monkey climb on the back of a wild elephant, and play on the ground with a ten-hooded snake. Then I saw him tread on a lion that was sleeping in the street. The lion opened its eyes, and raised its eyebrows. The monkey looked into the lion's eyes; and slowly the monkey grew bigger and bigger, until it was the size of the lion.

Allama Prabhu 101, 109, 211

The body as a temple

Since my body is a holy temple, why do I need another temple? No one ever asked for two temples. Is not a temple made of flesh superior to a temple made of stone?

Think of knowledge as day, ignorance as night, wisdom as jewels, and folly as leaves. The day is the face of the night, and the night is the face of the day. A necklace of the finest jewels lies buried in the face of the night. A tree in full leaf lies buried in the face of the day. When the necklace is fed to the tree, God is pleased.

When the hand grasps, the sky darkens; when the hand is open, the sky brightens. When the eye sees illusion, the sky darkens; when the eye sees truth, the sky brightens. When the heart remembers and resents, the sky darkens; when the heart forgives and forgets, the sky brightens.

Think of the soul as the sky, God as a toad, and ecstasy as a serpent. When the toad swallowed the sky, the serpent rose up. Then the serpent bit the person who was blind, and the person could see. No one has told the world.

Allama Prabhu 213, 218, 219, 277

Footsteps on water

Think of spiritual knowledge as a cat, worldly knowledge as a rooster, revelation from God as the sun, the power of action as a cuckoo, the mind as a casket, experience as a thread, the process of enlightenment as footsteps on water, and the vision of God as the sound of a word. The cat devoured the rooster; the cuckoo ate the sun; and the casket burned, leaving only a thread. No one can trace the footsteps on water; and no one can find the sound of a word by searching.

What is this darkness over my eyes? What is this death within my heart? What is this battle within my body? What is this revelling all around me? What is this path with which my feet are so familiar?

Think of the soul as the sky, ignorance as the desert, desire as a hunter, and life as a deer. The desert grew under the sky. In that desert a hunter roamed. He captured a deer, and carried it under his arm. The hunter will not die until the beast is killed.

I feel like a tree, with a fire burning within me. I feel like space, with a fragrant wind blowing. I feel like a wax doll melting. I worship the Lord, and forget the world.

Allama Prabhu 299, 316, 319, 396

The tree in the desert

Where the heart runs, the mind chases. Where God goes, the heart follows.

Think of the body as a city, the soul as a temple, knowledge as a hermit woman, the mind as a needle, the world as a cloth, and enlightenment as an ant. On the edge of the city a temple stands; and in this temple a hermit woman lives. In her hand she holds a needle; and with this needle she embroiders the world with beautiful patterns. One day an ant came, and devoured the woman, her needle, and the cloth.

Show me the teacher who can burn away the illusions that cover my eyes, and the desires that surround my heart. Show me the teacher who understands the first letter of God's word; that is enough for me.

Worldly people long to bury all shadows. But can shadows be buried while bodies remain alive? There is no point in hating what cannot be avoided. Worldly people do not understand the inner fabric of emotions and feelings.

Why do worldly people only pray to God when they are injured or dying? Does God become weary of listening to their groans?

Think of knowledge as a tree, the body as a tree, morality as fruits. Look! A tree is thriving in the desert, and on its branches luscious fruit is ripening. When the fruit falls to the ground, we shall eat it.

Allama Prabhu 429, 431, 451, 459,
492, 532

A million suns at dawn

One person dies, and a second person presides at the first person's funeral rites. Soon the second person dies, and a third person presides at the funeral rites. A man and a woman marry. Through the act of marriage grief becomes inevitable, because soon the husband or the wife will die, leaving the other alone. Lord, only your true devotees do not die.

I sat in darkness; I felt I was dressed in darkness. Then light came, and stripped away the darkness. God saw me naked.

There is one opponent that no hero can vanquish, and which vanquishes every hero. That opponent is sleep; sooner or later everyone is overcome by sleep. If sleep is so powerful, why do we ever doubt the power of God?

We say that a river runs — as if it were legs. We say that a fire consumes what it burns — as if it were a mouth. We say that a wind gathers up the dust — as if it were hands. The limbs and organs of God are everywhere.

Is God the body of all bodies, the breath of all breaths, the feeling of all feelings? Is God both near and far, both in here and out there? When I think of God, I exhaust myself.

I was looking for your light, and then I saw it. It was like a million suns at dawn. There is no metaphor for your light; it cannot be compared with anything else.

Allama Prabhu 629, 675, 699, 775,
802, 972

A woman's wealth

Do not forsake the sweetness of sugar cane, and taste only the bitterness of limes. Do not forsake the light of the moon and the sun, and set your affections on the light of a glow-worm. Do not give up wearing diamonds and rubies, and adorn yourself only with pieces of pewter. Do not abandon your search for the Lord, and devote yourself to lesser goals.

God is my life; the world tastes bitter to me. I love God only; let my eyes see no one and nothing but him. I want to live among the saints, who love God as I do; among the saints there is no corruption or intrigue.

Although I am a woman, I possess great wealth – given to me by God. My thoughts are a string of pearls, and my emotions are made of gold. My intellect is fashioned from diamonds, and my intuition from rubies. These treasures are kept in a casket; and the key to the casket is made of compassion.

Mirabai 44, 47, 49

The beauty of God's incarnation

God has been made flesh in the form of a man; and I am fascinated by his beauty. If he sees me in the bazaar or on the street, he teases me. His eyes are like lotus flowers; and when he glances at me, I feel weak. He has a herd of cattle which graze by the river; and he sits nearby playing his flute. I shall throw myself at his feet, and surrender myself – my heart and my body – to him. He is my Lord.

When my Lord goes away, I look out for him constantly; I long for him to return. My eyes ache from staring at the horizon. I cannot rest, and every night seems like half a year. No one can understand the pain of my separation; no one listens to my sorrow. I cry out: 'My Lord, when shall I see you? When will you make me happy again?'

When my Lord returns, he dances for my pleasure; yes, I have seen him dance. In his presence I feel no hunger or weariness; I want neither to eat nor to sleep. People mock me for my devotion to him; my relatives swarm around me like bees, and tell me I am foolish. But I do not care. I am the servant of my Lord; and serving him is my only desire.

Mirabai 51, 53, 54

Separation from God

Without God I cannot rest. The pain of separation from God is so great that sleep eludes me. Without the light of my beloved, my heart is dark; the light of a lamp cannot pierce the gloom. When I am apart from my beloved, I am plunged into lonely despair. I pass the night awake. When will my beloved come home?

The frog, the peacock and the sparrowhawk utter their cries; and the cuckoo calls out to the stars. The clouds gather, and lightning flashes. My body shakes with terror. My eyes burn to see him.

What shall I do, and where shall I go? Nothing can relieve the pain within my heart. Separation has stung me like a cobra. My life ebbs away, like a wave after it has broken. Prepare the herbs and spices with which to anoint my corpse.

Who will bring my beloved back to me? My Lord, when will you come back to see your most ardent lover? Nothing pleases my heart except your presence. When will you talk and laugh with me again?

Mirabai 56

A pedlar for God

There is a realm from which sorrow and pain have been banished. In this realm no one owns property, and no one pays taxes. There is no crime and no torture. No one is higher or lower in rank than anyone else, but all are equal. The food is delicious, and the drink is fine. People do whatever they want, and walk wherever they wish; no one ever challenges or questions them. This is the realm in which I wish to live; I and my companions will find it.

I journey along the road of life, with a feeble old bullock at my side, carrying my pack. The road is rough, hilly and overgrown. I am a pedlar for God. My pack is loaded with joy; this is the wealth which God manufactures and sells. I offer joy to all I encounter, in exchange for poison. I travel from the eastern shore to the western shore, and back again. Death will never ambush me with its stick, nor trap me in its snare. My skin is covered with an indelible red stain, so everyone knows who I am.

Human beings are like clay puppets. They look this way and that; they listen and talk; they dance and they run. They achieve some success, and swell with pride; then they fail at some venture, and their eyes fill with tears. Finally they die, and the clay is remoulded in another form. Life is a game; it is a magic show. I am in love with the one who controls the puppets, who performs the magic.

Ravidas 3, 4, 12

Nesting in the tree of existence

With what can I worship? All that should be pure, is impure. Can I offer milk? The calf has made it dirty with its slobbering mouth. Can I offer water? The fish have made it muddy. Can I offer flowers? The bees have taken all their pollen. Can I offer sandalwood? The snake has coiled itself around the sandalwood tree. Everything is tainted. But I can worship God with my body and my mind – and I can keep these pure. I shall abandon rituals and sacrifices, and offer only myself on God's altar.

We should not care what belongs to you, and what belongs to me; we nest only briefly on the tree of this existence. You may build a mansion as high as the clouds, with cellars as deep as the ocean; but nothing will alter the dimensions of your grave. You may curl your hair, and tie your turban with exquisite elegance; but your hair and your turban will soon be turned to ash. If you rely on the beauty of your spouse and your children, you have already lost the game of life. I know that my family is humble and my ancestry is despised; but I have always trusted in the Lord.

I have never known how to tan or sew leather – though people come to me for shoes. I do not possess a needle with which to make holes, nor a knife with which to cut the thread. Others stitch and knot – and tie themselves in knots. But I am free. I keep calling out to God, and death keeps his distance.

Ravidas 13, 19, 20

The lady of the house

Without the name of God, the universe is a lie. God's name makes the water in the sacred vessels holy. God's name makes the light of the temple lamp holy. God's name makes the garlands adorning the sacred statues holy. God's name makes the handiwork of the craftsman holy. God's name makes the whole world holy.

The day comes and the day goes; nothing remains the same. Relatives are born and relatives die; no family remains the same. Are you sleeping? Wake up, and see the one who cares for you – the one who feeds you and clothes you. Look within yourself, and you shall find his name written on your heart. So pray to him hour by hour. Abandon the notions of 'me' and 'mine', and cherish the name on your heart. Life is slipping away; soon it will be dark, and the world will be empty. Forget the world; it is only a display of magic. Love the magician.

A man builds a large house for himself, with a vast kitchen; but the time during which he occupies it, is soon past, and the house is vacant. My body is like a hut made of wood; at any time fire may consume it, and turn it into dust. But there is a lady living in this hut whom I call the soul. As the flames burn, she will run out of the hut, and survive. Robbers may kill my body and steal my possessions whenever they wish; but they cannot seize my lady.

Ravidas 23, 26, 27

Born to the highest rank

A family that has a true devotee of the Lord in its midst, is
neither high caste nor low caste; it is neither noble nor
humble. The world will know it by its fragrance. Priests and
merchants, warriors and craftsmen, peasants and labourers –
their hearts are all the same. But those who purify themselves
through loving God, exalt both themselves and their families.

Who could want anything but God? He has mercy on the
poor. He cares for those whom others find offensive. He
raises up the humble, and he shows no respect for worldly
power. He even exalts poets and mystics. I tell my friends
about him, and urge them to listen to what he says.

Let those who are proud of their birth, know that I too
am born to the highest rank – even though I work in leather.
My father is the Lord. I see his words on the leaves of trees.
I go round from house to house collecting the corpses of
animals, and people treat me with contempt; but in truth they
should bow down at my feet.

Ravidas 29, 33, 38

From a beggar to a servant

I have uttered lies as if they were truths; I have done evil as if it were good; I have thought wrong was right. People call me a servant of God, but I am a traitor to him. The power of God's name is so great that people treat me as a sage; but when they hear my words, they are listening to a fool. Let those who see and hear me, turn away from me; let them look directly at God, and listen to his guidance.

I was born into a family of beggars. Whenever my mother and father heard others celebrating, they cried with anguish. As a small child I went from door to door, weeping bitter tears, and asking for food. I had four goals in my life: to receive four morsels of food to fill my stomach. But I grew up to be a servant of God. When fate, the great astrologer, looks down on me, it feels cheated.

Is the name of God the sound of wisdom, or the sound of madness? It can construct a vast mountain from a scrap of straw.

Whenever people hear the name of God, and understand that name, they rejoice. There is no need for rituals in temples or in sacred rivers; understanding God's name is all that matters. Before they understand God's name, people are like beggars – craving even the water left over from making butter. But when they understand God's name, they are as rich as kings – spurning even the cream of the finest milk.

Tulsidas: Kavitavali 7.72, 73, 74

The power of God's name

There was a blind old man, who was mean, rude and harsh. He was walking along a lane, when a pig ran across the lane, and knocked him over. As he fell, fear gripped his heart. 'O God, O God!' he cried out. The impact of the fall broke many of the bones in his body. He lay on the ground for a few moments, groaning: 'O God, O God!' Then he died. In those few moments his meanness and rudeness and harshness were wiped away by the name of God; and he died in a state of union with God.

It is impossible to utter the name of God in a state of sin; it can only be uttered with love. And no one is so sinful that

they cannot utter God's name; even the most wicked men and women on this earth can turn to God's name, and his name will cleanse even the most stubborn of sins.

Tulsidas: Kavitavali 7.76

Vain ambition

'Tomorrow I shall have great wealth. Tomorrow I shall win a great victory in battle, and be acclaimed as a hero. Tomorrow the king will invite me to his court, and make me his chief minister.' So say men of ambition. Their ambitions are vain; even if their ambitions were fulfilled, the world would be no different, and they would be no happier. They are like a mosquito landing on a mountain, and declaring: 'My weight will make this mountain shake.'

In the past many wealthy, proud and powerful families have declined into humble poverty. At present many wealthy, proud and powerful families are declining. In the future many families will attain wealth, status and power – and then later decline. People see this, they hear this, and they know this; yet they do not truly absorb it.

The wise person says: 'Tomorrow I may die.'

Tulsidas: Kavitavali 7.120

A dark age

In this darkest of dark ages young people are no longer willing to study the sacred texts. Householders are no longer content with the work which their caste prescribes, but are gripped by ambition. Middle-aged people are no longer willing to withdraw from the world, and devote themselves to God. And old people refuse to spend their days in meditation and prayer. The right and proper order of human life has been tossed aside, as if it were a bundle of rubbish.

God is angry. His anger is expressed in the many diseases which are now prevalent amongst us, and in the frequent droughts which destroy our crops. Sick and destitute men and women cry out in agony and despair, but no one hears them or helps them. Why will people not learn the lesson of our present misery? Why will they not mend their ways?

I am frightened; I am terrified that I too might be struck down by some horrible illness, or be plunged into poverty. I turn to God for mercy. I praise him for his compassion. I beg him to protect me.

Tulsidas: Kavitavali 7.183

The joy of God's name

Let my tongue murmur: 'God, God.' Let my tongue repeat: 'God, God.' Let my tongue pray: 'God, God.'

Just as the rainbird yearns for clouds, my mind yearns to hear God's name; God's name is like a cloud of love. Just as wells, rivers, lakes and seas are useless for the rainbird, so any other name is useless to my mind; only the name of God can bring me peace.

Rituals and austerities may bear all kinds of spiritual fruits; but these fruits cannot satisfy the craving of my heart. A tiny morsel of God's name brings greater joy than all the worship in the world.

When thunder rolls and hailstones fall, the rainbird's love for clouds is tested; but when the rainbird passes these tests, its love is stronger than ever. When sorrow grips my heart and pain grips my body, my love for God's name is tested; but when I pass those tests, my love is stronger than ever.

God's name is my goal, and my means of attaining that goal. God's name fills me with love, and is the object of that love.

Tulsidas: Vinaya Patrika 65

The power of God's name

Speak the name of God, you fool. Repeat his name again and again. The name of God is your raft on the rough sea of life.

Only the name of God can ensure that you and your family live in comfort. Only the name of God has the power to make crops grow. In past ages this was understood; but in this sick age it has been forgotten.

The name of God brings blessings to good people and bad alike; it brings blessings to those who are right-handed, and to those who are left-handed. The name of God works for everyone.

For those who speak God's name, this world is like a beautiful garden filled with flowers and fruits; and life is like a feast in this garden. But for those who forget or ignore God's name, this world is like a desert; and there are only filthy scraps to eat.

Tulsidas: Vinaya Patrika 66

Love for God's name

Think of God's name with love.

It is provisions for your journey through life; and it is a companion who will travel beside you.

It is a blessing for those who are unblessed. It gives strength of mind and body to those who are weak.

It is a benevolent patron who buys food and clothing for the poor. It is a benefactor to those without a home.

It is a family to those who are alone. It is hands and feet to the disabled, and sight to the blind.

It is parents to orphans, and relatives to the destitute. It is land to those who own nothing.

It is a bridge which spans the river of existence. It is the source of unending joy.

God's name has no equal. It raises up those who have fallen. It makes the barren soil of my heart fertile.

Tulsidas: Vinaya Patrika 69

The moth, the fish, the dog and the frog

There is no one duller than me. My intelligence is below that of the moth and the fish. The moth is fascinated by a flame; and, ignorant of the danger, it flies into its heat. The fish is fascinated by bait floating in the water; and, oblivious to the danger, it catches its mouth on the hook. Like the moth I am fascinated by the flames of desire; like the fish I am fascinated by the bait of wealth. Yet such is my lack of wisdom, that I forget the dangers of desire and wealth. The wind of folly guides my flight through life; the river of stupidity carries me in its current.

I am like a dog lunging for an old bone. The bone is dry and cracked, with no meat or marrow to nourish the dog. So as it chews the bone, the sharp edges cut its mouth and draw blood. I chew on the pleasures which I once enjoyed; but now they merely injure my frail body. I am like a frog caught in a net. The more it struggles to break free, the tighter the net becomes. The net of worldly attachments surrounds my heart; and my religious activities merely worsen my plight.

My sins are too numerous to count; even God has despaired of keeping a record. God alone has the power to rescue me. In him I put my trust.

Tulsidas: Vinaya Patrika 92

Reality and fantasy

I am weighed down by a surfeit of delusion. When I look, I do not know whether I am seeing reality or fantasy; when I listen, I am beset with doubt and uncertainty.

On a hot day we often see a mirage of water ahead of us. If we believe that the mirage is genuinely a lake, our feelings of thirst are stimulated. So where does truth lie? The water is fantasy, but the thirst is real.

During a dream a man may think he is drowning in the sea, and he is gripped by fear. So where does truth lie? The drowning is fantasy, but the fear is real.

Life in this world brings pleasure and happiness to some, and pain and misery to others. So where does truth lie? Is this world really a place of happiness, or is it really a place of misery?

The sacred texts tell us the world is an illusion. Yet I am terrified of the world – and my terror is real. The sacred texts tell us that God is real. Only by devotion to God can my terror be turned to serenity.

Tulsidas: Vinaya Patrika 121

Guilt and fear

O God, I do not know what spiritual exercises I should perform. I know that I suffer from a severe spiritual ailment; but I do not know the medicine that will cure it. My ailment is that I cannot distinguish illusion and truth.

In a dream a king may imagine that he has killed a priest. The burden of this sin weighs him down, and he becomes desperate for forgiveness. He performs all kinds of sacrifices, but none wipes out his guilt. Until he awakes, the burden remains.

A man may have a garland put around his neck. But his eyesight is poor, and he mistakes the garland for a snake. He rips the garland from himself, and strikes it with a stick. He will continue to fear the snake is still alive, and so will continue to hit it with a stick, until he is utterly exhausted.

I am like the king, weighed down by the guilt of sins I have committed. But are those sins real or imaginary? I am like the man with poor eyesight, gripped by fear of illnesses, injuries and misfortunes that I may suffer. But is misfortune real or imaginary?

Guilt and fear are bound up with my sense of self. Until I root out this sense of self – until I cease to think of 'I', 'me', and 'mine' – I shall never be free.

Tulsidas: Vinaya Patrika 122

The vanity of eloquence

This much I understand, O God: that without your grace neither attachment nor delusion can be eradicated.

I am eloquent; but I have found that eloquence is vain. A lamp may seem to dispel the darkness of night; but in truth the darkness remains until the sun rises. In the same way skill in speech may seem to dispel the darkness of sin; but in truth the darkness remains until God appears.

Eloquence may be compared with the skill of a painter. A painter may produce a picture of delicious food, and show it to a hungry family. For a few moments the family may be happy, as if their hunger had been satisfied. But the pangs quickly return, and they are more miserable than before.

With my eloquence I can describe a life free from attachment and delusion; I can paint a picture in words of perfect joy and serenity. For a few moments I may make myself and my listeners happy, as if we had already attained such a state. But awareness of our true state soon returns, and we are more miserable than before.

As long as God's light does not shine in our hearts, our sorrow will persist. As long as God's grace does not nourish our minds, we shall have no comfort.

Tulsidas: Vinaya Patrika 123

False protection

You imagined yourself to be wearing perfect armour, that would protect you from every misfortune; you believed that you had no need of the Lord. But do you not know that death is constantly hovering overhead?

You have earned great wealth. You have purchased a large expanse of land; and in the middle of your land you have built yourself a magnificent house. You have a beautiful wife, and many sons and daughters. You have countless friends. But can you take your property and your family with you when you die? Can your friends shield you from death?

All your achievements in this world are merely reflections of your own delusion.

A king may conquer the world; he may turn every ruler in every land into his slave. Yet can he enslave death? On any morning death may come, and eat that king for breakfast. On any morning death may come and eat you.

Awake; open your eyes. See what is true; consider the teachings of the sacred texts.

I have opened my eyes; I have studied the sacred texts. Yet even now I fail to praise God as I should.

Tulsidas: Vinaya Patrika 200

Letters of petition

Who apart from you, O God, is my true patron? No one. I have reflected on this matter; and I have discussed it with people wiser than myself. And I have concluded that you alone are my master.

If anyone knows a being more powerful and more loving than you, let that person come forward.

A friend can be no substitute for you. The best of friendships is like the stitching between two pieces of cloth: if you pull gently, the stitching may hold; but if you pull hard, the stitching is liable to break. Some friends are like the false fruit in the heart of a banana tree; they promise much, but provide nothing. Or they are like cheap beads on a necklace, which only glisten when real jewels are put on either side.

I am the lowliest of your servants, O God. Please read my writings; they are letters of petition addressed to you. They come from the heart. Amend and correct them as you wish – and in response I shall amend and correct my heart.

Tulsidas: Vinaya Patrika 277

Hungry for truth

Tell me where I stand, divine Mother? Have you forgotten
me? Must I look for a stepmother, who will take me onto her
lap and comfort me? Are you putting a garland of dry bones
around my neck, and a tattered robe over my shoulders?

Is 'motherhood' no more than a word? Is there no reality
behind that word? Yes, you created me, and brought me into
being. But bringing a child to birth does not make a mother;
a mother is one who understands the pains and sorrows of
her child.

I am hungry, Mother; I am hungry for truth. Earthly parents
guide their children, teaching them how to behave, and telling
them what to believe. Why do you refuse to guide me?

Free me, Mother, from my misery; day and night I am the
slave of sorrow. You are my queen, and yet you have forgotten me, your most loyal subject. You have left me in the
noose of death, which tightens moment by moment.

Ramprasad 1, 2, 4

Divine injustice

Mother, by praising you I receive a double punishment. Even as I sing and pray to you, I feel the sting of your rejection. And far from answering my prayers with blessings, you respond with curses. Can I do anything that will please you? Is there any act of worship that will evoke your kindness?

Why are you so unjust? To those who are wicked, you give mansions in which to live, the finest food to eat, and elephants on which to ride. But to good people like me you give only hovels in which to live, and tiny patches of land on which to grow a few vegetables. The wicked wear robes of silk, while the good wear rags.

Mother, I do not want much. I want only to become dust under your holy feet – because your feet banish all sorrow and fear.

The vegetables from my land do not even feed my family, let alone me. So you force me to knock on the doors of those who are wealthy and wicked, and beg them for food. Do I deserve to be humiliated in this fashion? How can you treat your child so cruelly? Can a mother be the enemy of her child?

Ramprasad 6, 7, 8

Robbed of dusk

Mother, you have fed me with bitter food, assuring me that it was sweet. In my greed for sweetness I have eagerly taken what you offered; and now the taste in my mouth disgusts me. Your words have sounded sweet, but they turn bitter in the heart.

You have taught me games, which you promised would give pleasure. But when I have played them, they have brought nothing but misery. By following your guidance I have lost my wealth and honour, and am now treated with contempt. You have cheated me.

Mother, you dwell in my heart. Yet your heart is made of stone; only someone with a heart of stone could inflict such misery upon me. In you I thought I had a teacher who would reveal to me the truth. But you give me no peace. You have robbed me even of dusk: at night I am awake, as if it were day. Shall I ever sleep again; or has sleep been put permanently to sleep?

Ramprasad 10, 12

The end of the game

My game on earth is over, Mother. I have finished playing, and now death is close at hand. The fields and mountains of earth have been my playground, and now I am ready to leave.

Divine Mother, how should I prepare myself for death? What should I do in order to be saved? Cast me, Mother, into the waters of salvation. I do not want to be born again in this world; I do not want to enter the womb of another earthly mother; I want to be free from the cycle of birth, death and rebirth.

Through many lives I have wandered along the paths of error and folly. And as death has approached, I have trembled with fear at the prospect of rebirth. Free me from the chains of sensual passions which tie me to this world. Let me never again drink the liquor of desire; let me never again be drunk with greed and lust; let me drink instead the milk of serenity.

Ramprasad 61, 62, 63

By the fifteenth century Muslim invaders had conquered the whole of northern India, and were converting large numbers of Hindus to Islam. Sikhism sprung up as an attempt to reconcile the two religions. The term *sikh* simply means 'disciple'; and Sikhs are the disciples of the ten spiritual teachers – *gurus* – who guided Sikhism during its first two and a half centuries.

The first teacher, who founded Sikhism, was Nanak (d. 1539). He was the son of a Hindu tax official in the Punjab, in north-western India. From an early age he sought out the company of wandering ascetics, and at the age of thirty became a teacher. His teachings were influenced both by the Sufi mystics of Islam, and by the Hindu yogis of devotion. The hymns which he composed, form the basis of Sikh worship and spirituality.

Nanak chose as his successor Angad; and at his death Angad chose Amardas (d. 1574), who thus became the third guru. He in turn chose his son-in-law Ramdas (d. 1581), who founded Amritsar, the sacred city of the Sikhs. Both Amardas and Ramdas composed spiritual hymns in the style of Nanak.

One God

There is one God. Eternal truth is his name. He is the maker of all things. He fears nothing, and is the enemy of no one. He is immortal and unborn; he is his own being.

Repeat his name.

In the beginning he was the truth; and he has been the truth throughout all ages. Here and now he is the truth; and he will be the truth for all eternity.

Nanak: Japji Proem

Knowing God

It is not through thought that you can understand God –
even if you strive to grasp him with your mind a thousand
times. It is not through sitting in silence, engaging in
lengthy meditation, that you can reach the inner silence of
God. You cannot satisfy your hunger for God by amassing
great wealth – even the wealth of several worlds. If you possessed innumerable clever devices, none would assist you in
obtaining God.

How can you know the truth? How can you tear away the
veils of falsehood? By living in accordance with his will,
which is written on your heart.

Nanak: Japji 1

The will and power of God

Through his will God creates the forms of all things. But what is the form of his will? No one can describe it.

Through his will all forms are infused with the soul. Through his will some people have high places in society and some have low. Through his will people sometimes enjoy pleasure and sometimes suffer pain. Through his will some are graciously rewarded, while some must wander from birth to birth. Nothing is outside his will; all are subject to it. Those who are aware of the supremacy of God's will, are never guilty of pride.

If you believe in God's power, sing of that power. Sing of his many gifts, and the many signs of his love. Sing of his greatness, and his acts of kindness. Sing of his wisdom, which is hard to comprehend. Sing of the beauty of what he has made, and sing of how he destroys what he has made. Sing of how he takes life, and then restores it anew.

Sing of the infinity of God. Sing of how he is both far away and near. Sing of how he is both transcendent and immanent – far above us, and meeting us face to face. To sing truly of God would exhaust the vocabulary of every language; God is beyond all human expression.

Nanak: Japji 2, 3

The absolute truth

God is the absolute truth; his name is truth. The language of
God is the language of infinite love. People constantly pray to
him, asking him for more and more; and with unflagging
love he answers their prayers.

What should you offer, that you might see his kingdom?
What should you say, that you might please him? In the fragrance of dawn meditate upon him, glorifying his name and
reflecting on his greatness. He will put a robe of honour
upon you, and guide you to the gate of salvation. Thus you
will know that God is truth, that he is the source of all light.

God was not created, nor was his power established. He
exists by his own power. Those who worship him, are honoured by him. Sing his praises, and let his love flow into your
heart. Thus your sorrows will be swept away, and you will
be carried to the place of bliss.

Listen to the wise teachers who have heard God's word;
there are many such teachers. By their instruction knowledge
is acquired; and then you will know that God is everywhere.

Nanak: Japji 4, 5

Obedience to God

The condition of those who obey God, cannot be described. Those who try to describe it, are afterwards ashamed of their attempt. There is no paper and no pen which can be used to express the effects of obedience. God's name is pure; and those who obey God, know the joy of God within their hearts.

When you obey God, his wisdom and understanding enters your mind. When you obey God, you know all worlds. When you obey God, you are saved from all punishment. When you obey God, you are saved from death. Those who obey God, know the joy of God within their hearts.

When you obey God, your path through life is cleared of obstacles. When you obey God, you proceed along that path with hope. When you obey God, virtue becomes your companion on the journey. Those who obey God, know the joy of God within their hearts.

When you obey God, he guides you to the gate of salvation. When you obey God, your family also is saved. When you obey God, all who follow your example are also saved. When you obey God, you cease to be anxious about food and clothing. Those who obey God, know the pleasure of God within their hearts.

Nanak: Japji 12, 13, 14, 15

God's countless names

Countless are your worshippers, O God; and countless are
those who love you. Countless are your adorers; and countless are those who perform austerities for you. Countless are
those who read the sacred texts; and countless are the yogis
who are indifferent to the world. Countless are the saints who
meditate on your attributes; and countless are the sages who
strive to understand you. Countless are your true disciples;
and countless are those who do good works in order to please
you. Countless are those who think of you with love; countless are those who constantly fix their thoughts on you.
Human beings lack the power to describe you; but they can
strive to please you.

Countless are the fools who are spiritually blind; countless
are the thieves who devour the property of others. Countless
are those who oppress others weaker than themselves; countless are those who murder others for personal gain. Countless
are the sinners who pride themselves on the sins they commit; countless are the liars who relish falsehoods. Countless
are the slanderers who enjoy destroying the reputation of
others; countless are those who carry malicious gossip on
their heads. Human beings lack the power to describe you;
but they can strive to please you.

Countless are your names, O God; and countless are the
places where you are present.

Nanak: Japji 17, 18, 19

Singing to God

Where is the gate of your mansion – the mansion where you sit and watch over all things? How many musical instruments are played in that mansion? How many singers sing to you? Wind, water and fire sing to you. The angels sing to you. Sages sing to you. The virtuous and the patient sing to you. Heroic warriors sing to you. Teachers of philosophy sing to you. Beautiful young women sing to you. The continents which you have formed with your hands sing to you. The whole world sings to you.

They sing to you, the true Lord, whose name is truth. You made the world as it is, and as it shall be. You will never depart from this world, and no one can force your departure. You created all beings and all objects, giving to each its own colour and form. Your handiwork is a visible testimony of your greatness. You do whatever pleases you; no one can control you. You are the king of kings; all are subject to your will.

Nanak: Japji 27

Hail to the Creator

Make contentment and modesty your earrings, self-respect your purse, and meditation the ashes with which you smear your body. Make self-control your coat, faith your staff, and wisdom the path on which you walk.

Hail! Hail to God, the Creator. He is pure, eternal and indestructible. He is the same from one age to the next.

Make divine knowledge your food, compassion your larder, and the prompting of conscience the pipe with which you call people to eat. Regard the world as a thread, and the living beings in the world as jewels strung on the thread – making a divine necklace. Remember that God rules the world, allocating pleasure and pain according to his will.

Hail! Hail to God, the Creator. He is pure, eternal and indestructible. He is the same from one age to the next.

God sits in every part of the world, and he stores his blessings in every place. He looks upon his entire creation with love.

Hail! Hail to God, the Creator. He is pure, eternal and indestructible. He is the same from one age to the next.

Nanak: Japji 28, 29, 31

Human weakness and divine strength

I have no strength to speak, and no strength to be silent. I have no strength to ask, and no strength to give. I have no strength to live, and no strength to die. I have no strength to acquire wealth, and no strength to become indifferent to wealth. I have no strength to meditate on God, and no strength to contemplate his truth. I have no strength to find the way to escape from the miseries of this world. In God's arm there is strength; let him show me what he can do. In comparison with God no one is strong, because his strength overwhelms all human strength.

God created the days and the nights, the months and the seasons. He created wind, water and fire. And he created the earth as his temple. Within this temple he put living beings of every kind, and gave to each kind of living being its particular habits. He loves and honours all living beings, because all are made by his arm.

Nanak: Japji 33, 34

The realms of knowledge and happiness

In the realm of knowledge the number of winds and rivers and fires is known. The number of colours and forms is known. The shape and size of every living being are known. The number of mountains and regions and nations is known. The course of the sun and the course of the moon are known. The number of saints and kings is known. The languages spoken throughout the world are known. The quantity of things that can be known, is limitless; and in the realm of knowledge all are known.

From the realm of knowledge millions of joys and pleasures pour forth; and they flow into the realm of happiness. In the realm of happiness everything is beautiful, and nothing is ugly. Every living being in the realm of happiness acts in a beautiful fashion. No one can describe the beauty of the realm of happiness; and those who attempted to describe it, would feel ashamed of their efforts. In the realm of happiness there is limitless wisdom and skill.

Nanak: Japji 35, 36

God's palace

The Lord is perfect, and his throne is secure. Those who become holy, enter the palace of the Lord. The Lord's palace is beautiful beyond imagination; every wall is studded with rubies, pearls and diamonds. The palace is protected by a golden fortress; and around the fortress is a deep lake. Within the palace there is unending joy.

With what boat can you cross this lake, and with what ladder can you scale this fortress? The only boat and the only ladder is the guidance of a spiritual teacher. This guidance expels every kind of falsehood from the heart and the mind, and fills the heart and the mind with truth.

The Lord is wise, and his fields are fertile. He prepares the ground with his love, and then sows the seeds of his truth. The seeds bring forth an abundant harvest of joy.

How can you enter the Lord's fields, and share his harvest of joy? Only a spiritual teacher can show you the path which leads to those fields.

Nanak: Sri Rag

The hundred finest poets

Transform your heart, so that you sing God's praises with every breath you draw. Proclaim his greatness with every word you utter. All those who know the Lord, love him; and all who love the Lord, praise him.

God is infinite and eternal. His name is pure, and he loves every man, woman and child with the purest affection. His glory cannot be known by human minds; and human words cannot describe it. If the hundred finest poets in the world were gathered in one place, and were asked to express the glory of God, not a single line would be composed.

When God creates a living being, he does not need help, nor does he seek advice; and when he destroys a living being, he does not need help, nor does he seek advice. The Lord gives and the Lord takes away, as he chooses.

God is the source of all strength. He acts as he pleases, and causes others to act on his behalf. He looks on all people with favour, and blesses all people. He gives some a high status in the world, and some a low status; but in his eyes all are equal.

Nanak: *Ashtapadi*

The wife of the Lord

The perfect human being is like a wife to the Lord. She strips herself of all falsehood and hypocrisy, and adorns herself with honesty. She decorates herself with the words of a spiritual teacher. She is constantly available to him, with her hands clasped in prayer; and she begs him to take pleasure in her. She is besotted with love for him, and she honours him above all men. She dyes her hair with the colour of infatuation.

She calls herself the jewel of the Lord's crown. Nothing can break her love for the Lord; she is utterly at one with him. Her heart is saturated with his word; and her body is a living sacrifice, offered to him. She knows she will never be a widow, because the Lord was never born and will never die. Her beloved is an unending source of pleasure. He is constantly glancing in her direction, and smiles at her acts of obedience.

She combs her hair with truth, and she wears robes of love. She wears sandals of self-control. In her room she has the lamp of holiness constantly alight; and she wears God's name as her necklace. Her beauty reflects the beauty of the Lord, and her wisdom echoes his wisdom. She loves all people; but no one does she love more than her beloved.

Nanak: *Ashtapadi*

Loving God as water

Love God, as the lotus loves the water. The lotus loves the water so much that, whenever it is washed with water, it blooms. Those living beings which God created in the water, die without it; therefore they love the water. How can anyone be saved without love?

Love God, as the fish loves the water. The more the fish has, the happier it is, and the greater is its peace of mind and body. Without water the fish could not live for an instant; God knows what it needs.

Love God, as the duck loves the rain. When the rain falls, the duck rejoices. It leaps in the lake, and swims this way and that, watching it fill with raindrops. It loves to drink the pure rain as it falls from the sky.

Love God as water loves milk. When milk is boiled, the water within the milk sacrifices itself for the sake of the milk. The water evaporates and disappears, leaving behind a solid mass of pure milk. God welcomes the water, and honours it for its sacrifice.

Those who do not love God, do not see him; but those who love God, will meet him face to face. Those who do not love God, constantly make calculations, trying to ensure that their actions are profitable for themselves. Those who love God, simply do his will, knowing that God alone determines profit and loss.

Nanak: *Ashtapadi*

The nectar of God's name

God's name penetrates my heart. When I meditate upon God's name, I am happy; his name fills me with his perfect bliss.

The Lord preserves my health, as it pleases him; his name alone sustains me. The Lord guides my actions, as it pleases him; his name is my will. The Lord made me, fashioning my body and shaping my heart.

If my body were cut to pieces and burnt on a fire, God's name would lose none of its glory. If my heart were chopped up and thrown into a stove, God's name would lose none of its power. If I were to perform a thousand million religious ceremonies, I should add nothing to the glory and power of God's name.

How many opinions and theories there are about God! How many interpretations there are of his sacred texts! How many entanglements there are for the human heart! Truth alone is all that matters – the truth of God. Everything is inferior to the truth; and learning the truth is the highest of all activities.

Even if every man and woman were as high and mighty as a king, they would be low and humble in relation to God. Every man and woman was made by God; and they see by his light. By his favour every man and woman can obtain the truth; and his truth can never be erased.

Those who drink the nectar of God's name, will be satisfied for ever; their songs of ecstasy will resound for all time.

Nanak: Ashtapadi

Lasting wealth

We see mansions painted with bright colours; we see their gates decorated with rich carvings. They were built by people in love with the world, to give pleasure to their hearts. But soon these will fall into ruin. In the same way, the human body soon falls into decay, and returns to the dust. Remember, my brothers and sisters, you can take neither your wealth nor your body when you die.

God's name is the wealth that will last. Let God be your friend; then he will forgive all your sins. If God liberates you from the bondage of sin, then you will be liberated for ever. If God pardons your sins, then those sins have been wiped away for ever.

Do not regard your sons and daughters as your possessions; do not regard your spouse as your possession. If you regard them as your possessions, they will be a source of sorrow; but if you entrust them to God, they will bring you joy. Open your heart to God, and day and night you will be happy.

People pray for long life; no one wants to die. But pray instead for a happy life; pray for God to dwell in your heart, that he may fill you with joy. What use is long life without God? What use is the faculty of sight, if you do not see God is all that he has made?

As thirst is quenched by water, as the lotus cannot exist without water, as the fish would die without it, so the love of God alone can satisfy and sustain you.

Nanak: Ashtapadi

The ocean and the mountain

God's house is at the summit of a high mountain; the sides of the mountain are steep and rugged. But I have been shown the secret path, which is smooth and easy. The ocean of the world is rough and stormy; it is easy to sink beneath its waves. But I have been shown how to swim and remain afloat. I have received God's name.

If I merely utter God's name with my mouth, it will give me no help. But if I receive God's name in my heart, I shall be saved. If I merely acknowledge that I shall eventually die, then I shall die. But if I entrust myself wholly to God, then I am immortal.

A man may become an emperor ruling the entire world. He may have hundreds of thousands of armed soldiers under his orders. He may have elephants and horses without number. He may possess great storehouses filled with silver and gold. But he cannot stop his body decaying; every day and every night death is slowly crushing him under its feet. Without the name of God, what use is his wealth and power?

A man may have a beautiful wife, and many healthy children. He may wash his body in the finest oils, and wear the robes of silk. He may be treated with respect wherever he goes. But without the name of God, what use are luxury and honour?

Wealth and power, luxury and honour, are the waves on the ocean of the world. God's name alone can carry you to the other side – and show you the path up the mountain.

Nanak: *Ashtapadi*

The stages of life

In the first stage of life you love the milk of your mother's
breast. In the second stage you recognize your father and
mother, and love them. In the third stage you recognize your
brothers and sisters, and love them. In the fourth stage you
enjoy playing with friends. In the fifth stage you take great
pleasure in food and drink. In the sixth stage you are filled
with sexual desire, and marry. In the seventh stage you become a parent, and work hard for your children. In the
eighth stage your body is exhausted by work. In the ninth
stage your hair grows grey, and your breathing is difficult. In
the tenth stage you die; your body is burnt on the pyre, while
your relatives weep with grief.

Thus you come, you strive, and you depart, passing on to
your descendants only a name. Life is nothing – unless in the
course of it you learn the truth of God.

Nanak: *Majh ki War*

A hermit in the home

There are many people dressed in fine clothes, and possessing great wealth; but they have gained their wealth through deception, which has twisted their hearts and minds. But they will never find the palace of God; and as death approaches, they will be overwhelmed with despair.

Be a hermit within your own home. Study the writings of great spiritual teachers, and learn to control yourself. Think the truth, and speak the truth. And as opportunity arises, do good to others. If you conquer your heart with wisdom, your home will become God's palace.

When you go out, seek the company of those who are good and wise. God is their wealth; they trade in God's truth; his name is their merchandise. In each of their hearts God has built a vast storehouse of blessings.

To serve God is to love him. God is not served by hypocrisy; he hates every kind of lie and pretence. Servants of God clasp God to their hearts; they entrust themselves entirely to God's care; they root out from their hearts all pride.

Amardas: Sri Rag

The bird on the tree

How beautiful is the bird on the tree, who pecks at God's truth. It consumes the essence of God's name, and is happy. It has no desire to fly from one tree to another; it is content to remain in its nest.

Would that bird benefit in any way if it flew from tree to tree? Constant flying would wear it out, and make it miserable. It should remain on the tree where the fruit is divine. That tree never sheds its leaves; and its branches are always heavy with fresh fruit.

Amardas: Sri Rag Ashtapadi

At peace

Everyone longs for peace and rest; but it cannot be obtained without a spiritual teacher. Scholars grow weary of seeking knowledge in books, and astrologers grow weary of seeking knowledge in the stars; they wear fine clothes to signify their professions, but their efforts are useless. If God is merciful, he will give you a spiritual teacher who will show you the way to true knowledge; and from true knowledge comes peace and rest.

When you are at peace, music and song give pleasure; but when you are not at peace, music and song only worsen your condition. When you are at peace, prayer naturally springs up in your heart; but when you are not at peace, you cannot pray. When you are at peace, you constantly praise God, and never tire of contemplating him; but when you are not at peace, you contemplate material wealth.

God grants peace even to those who have gone astray – so long as they now find a spiritual teacher. Without the peace of God the world is dark; but with God's peace the world is radiant with truth.

The perfect teacher is God; and you should only follow a spiritual teacher who is in union with God. Under the instruction of such a teacher God's light will start to shine within you. You will praise God without limit; and you will possess wealth beyond limit – the wealth of his blessings.

Amardas: Sri Rag Ashtapadi

True love and true knowledge

Until you learn to love God, love for other people is no more than sentiment. Without knowing God, you cannot know other people as they truly are – so you cannot truly love them. Without seeing God, you are blind.

Every stretch of land and every object in the world is owned by someone; and at the moment of death we shall all lose our wealth. Men and women are besotted with love for material things; yet death is watching out for everyone.

Those whose hearts are full of deceit, cannot sleep in peace. Those who are attached to money, are haunted by despair. Those who never think of the one who made them and supplies them with food, will die and be reborn again and again; the noose of death will always be around their necks.

Those who follow the instructions of a spiritual teacher, will find happiness. Those who come to know God, also know themselves. Those who speak and act with honesty, are filled with God's peace. Those who regard all things as belonging to God, even their own bodies, are heard by God – and he answers their prayers.

People may worship God; they may practise various austerities; they may have perfect control of themselves. But unless the name of God is in their hearts, their efforts are worthless. Learn the name of God, and be filled by it.

Amardas: Sri Rag ki War

The company of saints

I meditate upon your name, O Lord. I keep the company of saints and sages, in whose hearts your name resides; and they have taught me how to keep your name in my own heart. I cannot reach you, nor can I see you; but I know you within me, and that knowledge brings me joy. All who know you within their hearts, are blessed.

I ask all I encounter about you. And if they reply that they know you, I kneel in front of them and wash their feet. I love to meet such people, and honour them; I love to pray with them, and to meditate with them on your name.

Wherever I look, I see you, O Lord. You pervade every heart, and you search every mind. You are with me at all times and in every place. There is one breath, which you have breathed. There is one matter, which you have created. There is one light, which you shine on all things. Yes, your light shines on all things, revealing the wonderful variety of what you have made.

Ramdas: Majh

Finding happiness

Beggars are happy when householders give them alms. The hungry are happy when they eat. Disciples are happy when they see their teacher, who will show them the path to God.

Grant me, Lord, a glimpse of you. Lord, you are the hope of my heart; you are my deepest desire. Have mercy upon me, and allow me to see you.

Birds are happy when they see the sun. Calves are happy when they are sucking milk. Disciples are happy when they see their teacher, who will show them the path to God.

All other affections are delusions; only affection for you, O Lord, is real. All other affections bring misery; only affection for you, O Lord, brings joy. All other affections are transient; only affection for you, O Lord, is permanent.

Mothers nourish their children, in the hope that they will grow up strong and healthy. I pray to you, O Lord, in the hope that you will reveal yourself to me.

Ramdas: Gauri

The farmer, merchant and shopkeeper

The farmer ploughs the earth and sows the seeds, hoping that his family will eat the fruits of his labour. I pray to you, O Lord, and repeat your name, in the hope that you will reward me and my family for my devotion. Save us, Lord, foolish and weak as we are. Make us do whatever is necessary to win your approval.

The merchant leaves home, with his horses loaded with goods, in the hope that he may exchange them for goods of greater value, and thereby increase his material wealth. I pray to you, Lord, and repeat your name, in the hope that you will increase my spiritual wealth.

The shopkeeper buys his wares from merchants, and sits in his shop dealing in them. His wealth is false; the pleasures which his wares promise, are false. Love of wealth is a snare, which prevents people from moving towards you, O Lord.

Let us be your slaves, O Lord. Bind us to you, that we may be free. Fill our minds with your name, that we may see light.

Ramdas: Gauri

Desire for God

Desire for you, O God, is always on my heart. When shall I
see you? I am a sinner, and have taken refuge at your gate.
My knowledge is useless, because it does not lead to knowledge of you. Transform my mind, that I may know.

Show compassion towards me, for you are the fount of
compassion. Forgive my sins, for you are the fount of forgiveness. I have gone astray; lead me back to the path of
righteousness. I am a silly child; give me wisdom.

Since I have never seen you, I feel separate from you; and
hence I grieve. I speak your name, but I have never entered
your presence; so I am weighed down with sadness. May I
meet you, Lord, face to face; and by this means I shall be
happy. When I see you, I shall live; while I do not see you,
I suffer a living death.

At present your name is my companion and my brother;
but I want to know the truth behind the name – I want to
know you. You are my life and my soul; you are my only
desire.

Ramdas: Gauri

To a stubborn heart

Stubborn heart, how can you ever know God? Stubborn and wretched heart, meditate on his name. Once you were clean, but now you have sunk into the mire of pride; once you were pure, but now you are corrupt.

Stubborn heart, search for God within you. He cannot be found by clever tricks and devices, but only through fixing your attention constantly on his name. Abandon every kind of hypocrisy and greed; only by leading a life of virtue can you find God.

Stubborn heart, through you alone can I find God. Rid yourself of all falsehood and superstition. Seek out a spiritual teacher, whose words are like nectar; the company of a saint will purify you. Listen to your teacher's instructions, and follow them.

Stubborn heart, break free from the net of sin in which you are trapped. Cut through the net by repeating God's name. Pray to God, begging him to look upon you with favour, and save you. If you are set free by God, then you are free for ever.

Stubborn heart, look for the light of God within your innermost depths. Look for God's treasures in your darkest places. Do not try to be clever or devious in your search, but be simple and innocent. You will find a gem whose sparkle can never be dulled.

Ramdas: Gauri Karhale

Enjoying God

Through spiritual devotion we propagate God's vine; and through spiritual devotion we learn to enjoy its fruits. There are countless delights in uttering the name of God.

God has implanted in every heart the desire to worship him; and he has implanted in every mind the need for a spiritual teacher. The spiritual teacher shows the disciple how every evil feeling and attitude may be rooted out from the heart, so the heart is made pure. Then the heart can fulfil its desire.

Religious ceremonies are not true worship. On the contrary, they often induce worldly pride, and so become an obstacle to worship. Elaborate rituals are like the dust which the elephant throws on its head after bathing.

Take pride only in winning God's approval; and God approves a heart that is humble and true.

Ramdas: Gauri ki War

BIBLIOGRAPHY

There are a number of translations of the works represented in the present volume. These are the most accessible.

Alphonso-Karkala, J. B., ed., *An Anthology of Indian Literature* (London, Penguin, 1971).

Bahm, A., tr., *The Yoga Sutras of Patanjali* (Berkeley, Asian Humanities Press, 1993).

Doniger, W., tr., *The Laws of Manu* (London and New York, Penguin, 1991).

Easwaran, Eknath, tr., *Bhagavad Gita* (London and New York, Arkana, 1986).

Easwaran, Eknath, tr., *Upanishads* (London and New York, Arkana, 1988).

Hawley, J. S. & Juergensmeyer, M., tr., *Songs of the Saints of India* (New York and Oxford, Oxford University Press, 1988).

Kingsbury, F. & Phillips, G. E., tr., *Hymns of the Tamil Saivite Saints* (Calcutta, Association Press, 1921).

Macauliffe, M. A., *The Sikh Religion, Volumes 1 & 2* (Delhi, S. Chand & Co., 1963).

Macnicol, M., ed., *Poems by Indian Women* (Calcutta, Association Press, 1923).

Radhakrishnan, S. & Moore, C., ed., *A Sourcebook of Indian Philosophy* (Princeton, Princeton University Press, 1957).

Ramanujan, A. K., tr., *Speaking of Siva* (London and New York, Penguin, 1973).

Thompson, E. J. & Spencer, A. M., tr., *Bengali Religious Lyrics, Sakta* (Calcutta, Association Press, 1923).

Tiruvalluvar, *The Kural*, tr. P. S. Sundaram (London and New York, Penguin, 1990).

Zarhner, R. C., tr., *Hindu Scriptures* (London, J. M. Dent & Sons Ltd., 1966).

The illustrations in this volume have been taken from Moor, E., *The Hindu Pantheon* (Madras, J. Higginbotham, 1864).

INDEX OF WRITERS